Katherine Mansfield,

Revised Edition

Twayne's English Authors Series

Kinley Roby, Editor
Northeastern University

KATHERINE MANSFIELD
by permission of the British Library

Katherine Mansfield,

Revised Edition

Saralyn R. Daly

Twayne Publishers • New York
Maxwell Macmillan Canada • Toronto
Maxwell Macmillan International • New York Oxford Singapore Sydney

Katherine Mansfield
Saralyn R. Daly

Copyright © 1994 by Twayne Publishers

Twayne Publishers
Macmillan Publishing Company
866 Third Avenue
New York, New York 10022

Maxwell Macmillan Canada, Inc.
1200 Eglinton Avenue East
Suite 200
Don Mills, Ontario M3C 3N1

Library of Congress Cataloging-in-Publication Data

Daly, Saralyn R.
    Katherine Mansfield/Saralyn R. Daly—Rev. ed.
        p.   cm.—(Twayne's English authors series; TEAS 23)
    Includes bibliographical references and index.
    ISBN 0-8057-7056-9
    1. Mansfield, Katherine, 1888–1923—Criticism and interpretation. I. Title.
II. Series.
PR9639.3.M258Z635   1994
823'.912—dc20   93-29509
                                                                                              CIP

10 9 8 7 6 5 4 3 2 1

Printed in the United States of America.

For Jan and Bruce, who deserve it again

Contents

Preface

When Twayne suggested that I rewrite *Katherine Mansfield*, I was at first ambivalent. Then Antony Alpers's enthusiastic description of the Newberry Library Mansfield Papers, in his selective edition of the stories, aroused my curiosity. Two years later I was able to spend a month at the Newberry, collating Mansfield first or early drafts with the major stories. Part of this book emerged from my speculations about clues to method and meaning that I found in those manuscripts.

I wrote my first *Katherine Mansfield* when the writer was out of fashion with the critics except for explications of a few stories. I wrote also in a frustrated awareness that the many personal texts through which she should have been sought misrepresented their subject. I used them as little as possible.

Much of that has changed, transforming sections of this book. There is still no scholarly biography or edition of the stories. But the collected letters, excellently edited, have been coming out since 1984 and should be complete by 1995 (Twayne generously let me delay this book until I could, scarcely moments ago, read volume 3). A steady stream of texts, frequently from New Zealand scholars, have enriched Mansfield devotees: her New Zealand publications, her unpublished work, expanded collections of her poetry and her critical writing, and a dialogic collection of letters between Mansfield and her husband, John Middleton Murry. She has found her feminist interpreters, and her pioneering and highly individual place in the modernist tradition has been convincingly delineated.

Though the overall structure of my revision remains that of 1965, it has been reworked in terms of what these new texts, critical treatments, and the Newberry manuscripts have stimulated in my thinking. In my brief biographical first chapter I have doubted, largely because of the letters, negative assumptions perpetuated, until recently, from Murry's testimony about her family relationships. Chapters 2 and 3 analyze her early work, and I confront the recurrent bee, the suspicion of plagiarism, that stirs up bonnets apparently unaware of deconstruction and the literary tradition.

Chapter 4 takes up Mansfield's avowed "turning point," evidenced in "Prelude" and "*Je ne Parle pas Français.*" I examine these with the help of manuscripts and the useful parallel text of "Prelude" and *The Aloe*. I could make chapter 1 brief because, with more letters and much of Murry's end of the correspondence available, I found it advisable to interweave biography throughout the book, describing the use Mansfield made of stories as messages to Murry—messages, incidentally, against which he seems incredibly obtuse or remarkably well defended. Either he did not acknowledge or he rarely, consciously, got her point. Thus I have come to believe that the *real* turning point occurred when Mansfield gave up writing to Murry, in time to create the great stories dealt with in chapters 5 and 6. There I discuss, as well, something of her form, methods (particularly as revealed in the Newberry Library Mansfield Papers "A Voyage" manuscript), and typical themes. Chapter 6, besides looking at Mansfield's formal development, critical ideas, and views on life, details more of her relationships with and influence upon Virginia Woolf and modernist short story form, and, in summary, reports some of the conclusions of recent feminist criticism.

Reluctantly, because of the cost of permissions, I deleted or paraphrased many exemplifying Mansfield quotations from what was intended as my final manuscript. The curious can find many of these excisions in my 1965 *Katherine Mansfield,* written in the halcyon days before the U.S. Copyright Act of 1976, when permissions for scholarly writing were freely given.

My bibliography is arranged to provide a chronology which distinguishes between publication by Mansfield alive and the posthumous publications by Murry. When they exist, I have substituted scholarly texts for Murry's idiosyncratic efforts. My brief account of manuscript collections is intended to stimulate curiosity and encourage further critical study. I no longer feel a need to remind readers of the vitality and depth of Mansfield's writing and its contemporary relevance.

Acknowledgments

I wish to thank the following for the reproduction of materials in this book: Oxford University Press for permission to quote excerpts from *The Collected Letters of Katherine Mansfield,* vols. 1–3, edited by Vincent O'Sullivan and Margaret Scott, © 1984, 1987, 1993, and from *The Great War and Modern Memory* by Paul Fussell, 1975; Random House, Ltd., the Hogarth Press Ltd., and the Estate of Virginia Woolf for permission to quote from *The Diary of Virginia Woolf,* vols. 1 and 5, edited by Anne Olivier Bell, copyright respectively © 1977 and © 1984 by Quentin Bell and Angelica Garnett; *Letters of Virginia Woolf,* vol. 3, edited by Nigel Nicolson and Joanne Trautman, copyright © 1980, by Quentin Bell and Angelica Garnett; St. Martin's Press, Inc., for permission to reprint excerpts from *The Critical Writings of Katherine Mansfield* by Clare Hanson, copyright © 1987, and *Short Stories and Short Fictions* by Clare Hanson, copyright © 1985; and the Society of Authors as representative of the Katherine Mansfield Estate for permission to quote from various writings by Katherine Mansfield.

I wish also to thank the British Library for permission to reproduce a photograph of Katherine Mansfield found in MS Add. 48970 at f. 228. I thank the Newberry Library for permission to reproduce two adjoining pages from Notebook 5 of their Mansfield Papers, for permission to quote excerpts from The Mansfield Papers in their collection, and for a Newberry Library Fellowship for in-residence study of those manuscripts. I also thank the National Endowment for the Humanities for a Travel to Collections grant, which helped support my work at the Newberry Library.

For generous assistance and unfailing hospitality it is a pleasure to thank the librarians and staff of the above libraries, as well as those of the Hoover Institute at Stanford University, Palo Alto, California; the language and literature library of the University of Tübingen in Germany; the Harry Ransom Humanities Research Center at the University of Texas in Austin; the Henry E. Huntington Library, San Marino, California; the University of Illinois Library at Urbana; and the University of California Research Library and the California State University Library, both in Los Angeles.

I also thank my former colleague and friend, Sharon Bassett, for last minute bibliographic assistance and my enduring friends at the University of Illinois in Champaign-Urbana, Jan Lawson Hinely, for her patient, acute, and painstaking reading of sections of the book-in progress, and her husband, R. Bruce Hinely, for gourmet sustenance and challenging space-age recreation along the way.

Chronology

1888   Katherine Mansfield born 14 October in Wellington, New Zealand, third daughter of Harold Beauchamp and Annie Burnell (Dyer) Beauchamp.

1895–1898   Attends Karori State School, Wellington, New Zealand.

1898–1899   Attends Wellington Girls High School, Wellington, New Zealand. Is published twice in the *High School Reporter*.

1899–1900   Attends Miss Swainson's private school, Wellington, New Zealand. Is published in *Comet*.

1903–1906   Attends Queen's College, London. Five sketches are published in *Queen's College Magazine*. Meets Ida Baker (LM). Returns to New Zealand.

1907   Three sketches and a poem are published in the Melbourne *Native Companion*. Camping trip, *Urewera Notebook*.

1908   "Study: The Death of a Rose" is published in *Triad*. Returns to London. Has love affair with Garnet Trowell.

1909   Marries George Bowden 2 March; leaves him the same day. With Trowell, becomes member of the chorus of a traveling light-opera company. Pregnant, is lodged by her mother in the spa, of Bad Wörishofen, Bavaria. Has a miscarriage.

1910   Returns to London; lives briefly with her husband. February, March, May, July, and August publication in the *New Age*. Has abdominal operation; rheumatic fever.

1911   May, June, August, September, and October publication in the *New Age*. In July suffers from pleurisy in Bruges, Belgium, and Geneva, Switzerland. In September returns to London. *In a German Pension* is published in December. Meets John Middleton Murry.

1912   In March publication in the *New Age*. In spring "The Woman at the Store" is published in *Rhythm*. In April Murry moves into Mansfield's flat. In May travels to Paris with Murry. In fall Stephen Swift, publisher, vanishes, leaving *Rhythm* debts.

1912–1913   Is coeditor of *Rhythm,* June to March. Many publications.

1913   In March last issue of *Rhythm*. In May–July four stories published in the *Blue Review,* which then fails. Meets D. H. and Frieda Lawrence. Works as a film extra. In December is in Paris and writes "Something Childish But Very Natural." Meets Francis Carco.

1914   In February returns to London. In October lives near D. H. and Frieda Lawrence, near Cholesbury.

1915   In February her brother Leslie Beauchamp is in London to join his regiment. Mansfield makes three trips to Paris, staying in Francis Carco's flat. Begins *The Aloe*. On 7 October Leslie Beauchamp is killed at Ploegsteert Wood. In October and November three stories are published in four issues of the *Signature,* which then fails. In November begins residence in Bandol, France. On 4 November "Stay-Laces" is published in the *New Age*.

1916   In April lives in North Cornwall near Lawrence. In May moves to South Cornwall. In fall returns to London. Meets Garsington circle and Virginia Woolf.

1917   May, June, September, and October publication in the *New Age*. *The Aloe* rewritten as *Prelude*. TB diagnosed.

1918   In January resumes residence in Bandol. On 19 February has first hemorrhage. Writes "Je ne Parle pas Français." In March is in Paris, caught with LM in the "Big Bertha" bombardment. In April returns to London. On 29 April is divorced by George Bowden. On 3 May marries Murry. In June *Prelude* is published by the Hogarth Press. On 8 August her mother dies. "Bliss" is published in the *English Review*. Moves to Hampstead with LM housekeeper.

1919   Murry becomes editor of the *Athenaeum*. Mansfield begins book reviews for the *Athenaeum*. In

April–August poetry published in the *Athenaeum* under pseudonym Elizabeth Stanley. In April–October Chekhov letters, translated with Koteliansky, are published in the *Athenaeum*. In September begins residence in Ospedaletti, Italy with LM. In December sends "The New Husband" verses to Murry. Murry comes for Christmas.

1920   On 11 January writes "The Man Without a Temperament." In January moves to Menton, France. In April returns to London. In June–December publication of stories in the *Athenaeum*. In December *Bliss and Other Stories* published by Constable. In September returns to Menton, France, with LM. In October–December writes "The Life of Ma Parker," "Miss Brill," "The Young Girl," "The Stranger," "Poison," "The Daughters of the Late Colonel," and other stories.

1921   On 26 February "The Life of Ma Parker" published in the *Nation*. In May begins residence in Switzerland. In July is living with Murry, LM nearby at Montana, Switzerland. In July–January writes "At the Bay," "The Garden Party," "The Doll's House," "A Cup of Tea," "Marriage à la Mode," "Her First Ball," "An Ideal Family," "Mr. and Mrs. Dove," "The Voyage," and other stories.

1922   In January "At the Bay" is published in the *London Mercury*. In February "The Garden Party" is serialized in the *Westminster Weekly Gazette;* in Paris with LM for radium treatment for tuberculosis; "The Doll's House" is published in the *Nation;* writes "The Fly"; *The Garden Party and Other Stories* is published by Constable. On 18 March "The Fly" is published in the *Nation*. On 29 April "Honeymoon" is published in the *Nation*. In May finishes first course of radium treatments. In June returns to Sierre, Switzerland. In July writes "The Canary." On 14 August makes her will, naming Murry literary executor. In August returns to London. In August–September translates, with Koteliansky, Gorki's *Reminiscences of Leonid Andreyev*. In September undergoes second course of radium treatments. On 16 October enters the Gurdjieff Institute, Fontainebleau, France.

1923   On 9 January dies of a hemorrhage. Is buried 12 January in the Protestant cemetery, Avon, Fontainebleau, France.

Chapter One

"Out of This Nettle, Danger"

The observable elements that molded Katherine Mansfield (née Kathleen Mansfield Beauchamp) are those which seem to have shaped many artists—conflicts with environment, rootlessness, a permanent sense of alienation. Less than three years before her death she composed an oddly revealing "Biographical Note":

> Née 14 October à Nouvelle Zélande
> Premier voyage age de six mois
> Premier histoire publiée age de neuf ans
> Le reste de ma vie est passé en voyagant et en écrivant les "short stories." . . .
> Wife of the brilliant poete et critique J.M.M. who is the famous editor of the newly brought to life and prominent Athenaeum
> Two cats.[1]
>
> —K.M.[2]

The brief mention of the cats laconically minimizes the excessive, perhaps teasing flattery of John Middleton Murry. But the rhythms of repeated structures and echoing words, even in this whimsical record, are those of the practiced writer who reveals what she chooses of her image. "Premier voyage . . . Premier histoire . . . ," she writes, and then, "Le reste de ma vie . . . voyagant . . . écrivant. . . ." First trip . . . first story . . . wandering and writing. Thus she had spent her life. These were the things she had done, and like it or not, these were the things that had mattered. So, toward the end, Mansfield set down her homelessness as though, from the beginning, it had been interwoven with her writing.

Biography, like autobiography, involves selection and speculation. Sophisticated writers, reshapers of reality as they have known it, work in consciousness of their fiction. Asked to write of herself, Mansfield treated the request with a factual frivolity that pleased and served her purpose for the moment. It would not have surprised her that 60 years after her death, no adequate biography has yet been written. That her husband, Murry, got it wrong she would have understood as appropriate to his psychological makeup. The distortions of later biographies reflect, for the most part, the male-defined interests her writing often described and denounced.[3]

In Mansfield's account much has been omitted. Had she not wished to flatter Murry, she might have added adventurous young bohemian, destroyed too soon by inadequately treated disease, by the financial neglect of her wealthy but stingy father, and by the superficiality of her dependent, pretentious, parsimonious husband. Though not before she turned these disadvantages into literature.

She often used her memories to create fiction, but her stories are not transcripts of her life. The biographies consistently confuse the two. The least tampered with sources of information are the new edition of her letters, as yet published only through April 1920, with two more volumes promised by 1995, and the Hankin letter editions, which fill the lacuna.

The stories are consciously wrought fictions, sometimes messages, usually to her husband, John Middleton Murry, abstracted from disappointments she was experiencing; sometimes testaments to her beliefs; but not confessions, not autobiographical. Narratives about happy, unconflicted characters, even children, lack fictional interest because they are unproblematic; they lack tension and resolution. Writers must generally draw on their experience for material, but they are artificers, not "truth" tellers.

Mansfield grew up in and enjoyed an affluent environment. She was nurtured by her parents in varying degrees, as many of us are, and also by her maternal grandmother. She was born Kathleen Mansfield Beauchamp on 14 October 1888, reputedly on a very windy day, in Wellington, New Zealand. Her father, Harold, was a successful, ambitious merchant, soon to become a director of the Bank of New Zealand. With Kathleen's arrival, the delicate beauty, Annie Burnell Beauchamp, née Dyer, had borne three daughters in four years of marriage. She would bear two more girls, one of whom died before Kathleen was three, and finally, when Kathleen was five and a half, a boy.

Harold Beauchamp grew increasingly affluent, able to support in style not only his wife and five children but also his wife's mother and sister, and for a time two sisters. The girls attended Wellington Girls High School, where Kathleen contributed stories to the school magazine, the first when she was nine. At the end of 1899 she won school prizes for English, arithmetic, and French. Next the sisters attended Miss Swainson's private school for girls, where Kathleen contributed to a magazine of stories and jokes. As is not unusual in schools, her humor and creativity were evidently offensive, at least to Miss Eva Butts[4] and

Mrs. Smith, whose unpleasant, schoolmarmish criticisms Alpers saw fit to record as indications that Kathleen was a misfit (Alpers, 19). Music lessons on the cello resulted in more intimate acquaintance with the family of her teacher, Tom Trowell, friendships which would lead, when she grew older, to two failed romances, pregnancy with a miscarriage, and an unconsummated marriage to George Bowden, another music teacher. But this gets ahead of the story.

When she was 14, her father hired the entire passenger space of a freighter to take the family to London, where he enrolled her and her two older sisters in Queen's College. It was a new world. Soon Kathleen began what would be a lifelong, love-hate friendship with Ida Baker, whom she nicknamed LM.[5]

Mansfield wrote later that she learned little in her three years at Queen's, where she dreamily and romantically absorbed the atmosphere: "My college life . . . might never have contained a book or a lecture. I lived in the girls, the professor, the big lovely building, the leaping fires in winter and the abundant flowers in summer. The views out the window, all the pattern that was—weaving. Nobody saw it as, I felt, I did."[6] Nevertheless she did well in French and German, continued to publish stories in the school magazine, and internalized Professor Walter Rippmann's admiration of Walter Pater, Oscar Wilde, and other fin de siècle writers.

After three years of cultural explorations in London, the sisters returned to Wellington. Not only Kathleen but both her sisters found New Zealand provincial, as, of course, it was. "They can't wait to get back to England," recalled one observer. None of them married a New Zealander (Tomalin, 32). Since Mansfield kept a journal and wrote letters that people saved, we read of her intense desire to leave. The sisters, whose voices we lack, eventually left as well; their Aunt Belle, who had accompanied them to London, married there and remained when the sisters were taken home by their father.

Mansfield found much to enjoy during her interlude at home: parties, dances, retreats to the family beach cottage at Day's Bay, fascinating friendships, courting young men (five proposed marriage), expensive new clothing, a continuation of her cello lessons with Tom Trowell, the comforts of a bank director's home. More strenuously she went on a rugged camping trip, exploring the New Zealand "out back."[7] She also attended typing and bookkeeping classes, read widely, and worked at her writing. Eventually, through a contact made by her father, she sold her first "Vignettes," modeled on those of Oscar Wilde.

Earnestly she copied into her notebooks the advice of her masters or
composed on their models:

> "To be premature is to be perfect."—O.W. [Oscar Wilde]
> "To acknowledge the presence of fear is to give birth to failure."—K.M.
> [She had chosen her penname by this time.]
> "The strongest man is he who stands most alone."—Henrik Ibsen.
> "Push everything as far as it will go."—O.W.
> "No life is spoiled but one whose growth is arrested."—O.W.
> "If you want to mar a nature, you have merely to reform it."—O.W.
> "The only way to get rid of temptation is to yield to it."—O.W.
> "To realize one's nature perfectly—that is what each of us is here for."—
> O.W. (*Journal*, 2–4)

As time went on, various plans for the return to London were proposed and then canceled. When one failed, another soon emerged. In
March 1908 she wrote her sister Vera, then in Sydney, "my Mrs Weston
plan has fallen through. Now I am not conquered yet. . . . Mother has
the plan of sending us to London to live together—we three in a flat on
£300 a year" (*Letters*, 1:42). Finally her father was persuaded. On 9 July
1908 she sailed for London with an allowance of £2 a week.

For years Mansfield had thought she was in love with the rising
young musician Tom Trowell (later called Arnold). When the passion
was not reciprocated, she turned to a more successful affair with his
brother Garnet, whom she expected to marry. Around the end of the
year Garnet's father, her old music teacher, objected to the match. In
February 1909 she was introduced to a tenor singer, George Bowden,
who taught speech and singing in various London divinity colleges. He
was 11 years older than Mansfield. After a month of mocking his passionate love letters, on 2 March she unaccountably[8] married him and as
suddenly left him on the evening of the wedding. Soon after she rejoined
Garnet, who was traveling with the Moody-Manners Opera Company.
She became a member of the chorus (Alpers, 82–89, 92).

By May there was no doubt that she was pregnant. Her mother had
long since embarked from New Zealand to investigate the marriage. She
arrived 27 May and carried her daughter off to Bad Wörishofen, a fashionable Bavarian spa, where she soon left her aberrant daughter. By the
end of the year Mansfield suffered a miscarriage. This mischance, however, in that it sent her to Bavaria, was of literary benefit, for there she
may have read for the first time short stories by Anton Chekhov, whose

work confirmed her developing artistic instincts. And in Bavaria she made the observations which became the stories of *In a German Pension*.

Though Annie Beauchamp, on her return to New Zealand, took Kathleen out of her will, there was apparently no break in their relationship. Mansfield sent her mother affectionate postcards from the spa (*Letters*, 1:93). They never ceased to correspond. When in 1918 her mother died, Mansfield remembered her with admiring appreciation. The fictional portraits modeled on her mother constitute feminist portrayals of a woman's resistance to the conventional expectations of marriage: sexual intercourse at the will of the husband, childbirth, child care, household duties. Linda Burnell in "Prelude" and "At the Bay" provides a mouthpiece for Mansfield's mature views.

Back in London in 1910, Mansfield began what seemed to be a successful literary life. Her sardonic, immature stories appeared regularly in the *New Age*, a socialist publication intent on challenging a world still reminiscent of Queen Victoria. Later a meeting with John Middleton Murry drew her even more into an artistic milieu. She experimented in various story forms, too often writing to suit the editorial policies of the magazines—*Rhythm*, the *Blue Review*, and *Signature*—she and Murry edited between 1912 and 1915.

The *Blue Review* ended in financial collapse in 1913, shortly after a friendship with D. H. Lawrence had begun. At the end of the year Murry assumed that he could make a living reviewing French books from Paris for the *Times Literary Supplement*. Almost as soon as they had moved there, with all of their furniture and some of Ida Baker's, Murry's expectations and his nerve failed.

When he was called back to London to face bankruptcy court, he did not return to Paris as promptly as promised. A series of letters tell the story. On 10 February 1914 Mansfield wrote, "Your room is ready for you." The next day a realistic letter revealed her sympathetic awareness of Murry's insecurity and ambivalence: "I do not think that it is any good you staying anywhere if you are worried about money. . . . What is at the back of your darling mind? . . . Tell me quite plainly, won't you? Did you take a return ticket? Would you rather stay on now and save the money and manage things by letter?" By the time he came back to Paris the venture was over. On 24 February she described to Ida the "Last Moments" in the flat. Murry had returned to help sell "even the bedding" (*Letters*, 1:136–39).

Probably the first clear revelation to Mansfield of Murry's inadequacy came with the fiasco of the Paris flat. He had gone to Paris to forsake journalism but could not resist the security of a £6-a-week job on the *Westminister Review*. In the interval of decision while she waited in Paris, Mansfield, untied to any editorial policy, wrote her first long story, "Something Childish But Very Natural." It was a message to Murry, the first of many stories of betrayal.

During these years her uneasy alliance with Murry became permanent. Their life together, however, never left Mansfield with the feeling that she at last had roots. Instead, the interruptions of their relationship by her need to travel for the sake of health probably intensified her loneliness. Gradually she discovered, too, that amid London's bohemia and in much of Murry's world she remained alien. Entries in her journal of spring 1914 are characteristic: "And I am sure J. [Murry] could get a great deal of pleasure out of pleasant society. I couldn't. I've done with it, and can't contact it at all now. I had so much rather lean idly over the bridge and watch the boats and the free, unfamiliar people and feel the wind blow. No, I hate society." A few days later she wrote: "I feel a real horror of people closing over me. I could not *bear* them" (*Journal,* 58).

In August, as World War I began and Murry rushed to enlist and then hastened as swiftly to obtain a medical rejection, Mansfield wrote in a notebook, "I do not trust Jack. I'm old tonight. Ah, I wish I had a lover to [illegible; Alpers, 168, reads nurse] me, love me, hold me, comfort me, to stop me thinking" (*Journal,* 61). By December she was fed up and added, "For him I am hardly anything except a gratification and a comfort. . . . He doesn't know me—or want to. . . . Jack, we are not going to stay together. . . . What we have got each to kill—is my *you* and your *me*. . . . [L]et's do it nicely" (*Journal,* 63).

In spring 1915, increasingly dissatisfied with Murry's passivity, she made an illegal trip to the French front to visit the young writer Francis Carco. The result was another long story, "An Indiscreet Journey." Neither of these works seems designed for any audience then available to Mansfield. Neither was published in her lifetime, but both marked a distinct technical and emotional change in her writing, and "An Indiscreet Journey" evidenced her developing social consciousness under the impact of World War I. Shortly after the completion of the latter story she began *The Aloe,* a novel drawing on her New Zealand experiences.

In the looser form of these stories Mansfield let extended detail reveal by implication meanings more sympathetic than she had usually attempted. After the death of her brother Leslie in October 1915, she asserted in her journal, "I feel I have a duty to perform to the lovely time when we were both alive. I want to write about it" (*Journal,* 90). Her work did not continue in that vein. She struggled with *The Aloe* during 1916 but could not turn it into the sensitive and perceptive *Prelude* until the summer of the following year. Meanwhile she returned to her terse, sardonic *New Age* manner. One story appeared in that publication in 1915 and 10 between May and October 1917. While at work on the deeply caustic "Je ne Parle pas Français" in February 1918, she excitedly described this story as her technical turning point (*Letters,* 2:56, 72–73). Clearly, in this indecisive period, she was artistically homeless as well as emotionally bereft.

Before the war ended, the pattern of her life was established. Every winter since 1914 she had suffered illness of some sort,[9] and there had been a sojourn in France, sometimes on the doctor's advice. On 19 February 1918 she had her first tubercular hemorrhage. Fortunately Ida Baker, the friend from Queen's College days, was on hand to care for her. They continued an ambivalent relationship as illness intensified and the necessity of Baker's help deepened Mansfield's resentment of their codependency. Together in March and April they endured the "Big Bertha" bombardment of Paris and other wartime constraints before they could obtain the documents necessary for their return to England.

Then, freed after nine years by the divorce Bowden had secured, Mansfield was able to marry Murry on 3 May, but within two weeks she had to leave him for the sake of her health. At the end of June they were together again, and so the pendulum continued to swing. Incessantly wandering in search of a healthy climate, lamenting her aloneness when she must part from her husband, she disciplined herself to see more clearly, to write better, "truer" stories.

Her literary career became solidly established. *Prelude* was published in 1918 as a small book by the Hogarth Press, and Mansfield began an uncomfortable acquaintance with Virginia Woolf. Each found the other the only woman worth talking with about writing. But malicious Bloomsbury gossip, Mansfield's frequent absences abroad, and Woolf's regrettable and regretted jealousy impeded their friendship.

The *English Review* published "Bliss" in June. When, that winter, Murry became the editor of the *Athenaeum,* his wife became a regular book reviewer. She also contributed, with S. S. Koteliansky, translations of some Chekhov letters. In June 1920 the *Athenaeum* began to publish stories: Mansfield supplied eight by December and wrote three more for other magazines. *Bliss and Other Stories,* published in December of that year, received favorable critical comment. Though Mansfield was by no means satisfied with her work, she had arrived. Praise and criticism usu-

ally reached her by mail, for with the increasing seriousness of her tuberculosis, she could rarely risk living in the English climate. In this state of
physical remoteness, her fictional world became more vividly and more
complexly realized.

Despite—perhaps because of—her illness, her story output grew
almost feverish. Between November 1920 and July 1922, 21 months,
she completed her work with at least 20 stories, a number of fragments,
and the beginning of a novel. Many of these found instant periodical
publication and were then collected in *The Garden-Party,* which appeared
in February 1922. There were two tremendous spurts: between October
and December 1920 Mansfield wrote eight stories, among them six of
her finest; again from July to December, 1921, while living with Murry
in Switzerland, she wrote 12 stories, some to fulfill a contract with
Sphere. Though in her letters she belittled the *Sphere* stories, her concern
with style and structure was constant. She judged each creation severely.
In February 1922 she wrote "The Fly," and she was planning another
volume while she underwent a new series of radium treatments in Paris.
In July, back in Switzerland with Baker while Murry lived nearby and
visited her on weekends, she wrote "The Canary," her last completed
story.

The next month Katherine Mansfield made her will, in which she
instructed Murry to destroy her unfinished work and personal papers.
That he did not is a service to the literary critic, but the fragmentary
manner in which he released her "remains" served only to create a confused image of the developing artist.[10] In London Mansfield underwent
a second course of radium treatments, but she had lost faith in their effi-
cacy. Instead, she decided, she must cure herself by mystic means. With
this in mind, she returned to France and in October entered the
Gurdjieff Institute at Fontainebleau.[11]

On 9 January 1923 Murry came for a belated holiday visit. Mansfield
was radiantly happy with him during the afternoon and evening. Then,
as she started upstairs to bed, a violent hemorrhage began, and within a
few minutes she was dead. The Shakespearean epigraph she used on the
title page of *Bliss* serves for her tombstone inscription: "But I tell you,
my lord fool, out of this nettle, danger, we pluck this flower, safety."[12]

From the experience of her 34 years Katherine Mansfield shaped her
stories. Her time and scope were limited. But—when with illness the
scope decreased and the time, she knew, shortened—her production
intensified and her utterance deepened. In 1908, as she began an inde-

pendent life in London, her writing merely reflected her feeling of home-lessness. In this she heads a long line of twentieth-century writers who cannot go home again, but whose imaginative will often returns. To her, as to many, adventures in bohemia proved painful.

In self-defense the little colonial learned but was not deceived by the brittle mask of sophistication. The overdone satiric recoil characteristic of *In a German Pension* and of "Sunday Lunch" measures the extent of her pain. Apparently she never completely learned to protect herself. During tea one April afternoon in 1919, Virginia Woolf observed that she was "oddly hurt. . . . Her hard composure is much on the surface."[13] Yet Mansfield had by that time completed in "Bliss" the exploratory appraisal of the world that revolves around the arts, and by the end of 1921 she would record her conclusions in "Marriage à la Mode."

She remained uncomfortable among the intelligentsia she called the "Blooms Berries." It was not intellectuality that she found offputting. She enjoyed many months of conversation with the philosopher and political activist Bertrand Russell, who acknowledged that he found her mind "interesting" (*Letters*, 1:284–88, 293–97). But Mansfield was more absorbed in individuals and natural beauty than in painstaking analysis of vague abstractions.

D. H. Lawrence's 1914 escapist project of founding an ideal commu-nity on an island was discouraged by Katherine Mansfield of New Zealand, who confronted him with statistics on actual island life. She would often record at great length the remarks of a humble maid or gar-dener, but the endless, abstract philosophical and spiritual conversations of Murry with J. D. Fergusson, Gordon Campbell, or Lawrence she found unprofitable. Practicality, openness, simplicity touched her heart, as did the beauty of flowers or the sea. A notable characteristic of her work was always immediacy of sense impressions and individualized response to them. Months after Mansfield died Virginia Woolf recalled that she "possessed the most amazing *senses* of the generation so that she could actually reproduce this room for instance, with its fly, clock, dog, tortoise if need be, to the life."[14]

In two years of steady work reviewing books for Murry's *Athenaeum*, Mansfield essentially wasted herself and earned a little money. She com-plained that Murry sent her only mediocre novels. Her critical theory emerged in bits and pieces, as much in her letters as in her reviews. Clare Hanson has described Mansfield's reviewing technique: she "suggests indirectly what might be tactless as forthright statement." An image of the work reviewed is thus evoked. A deadpan retelling of a story can ridicule it by indirection. Often a review opens with a rhetorical question and ends with a "suspended conclusion." Mansfield's critical persona is "androgynous-tough, 'masculine' and fearless . . . yet capable of the finest (feminine) judgments and discriminations. A prevailing note of irony dissolves tensions between male and female, writer and work." The losses and disillusionments of World War I intensified her insistence that art should have a serious ethical dimension.[15]

Toward the end of her career, in a letter to the young, aspiring writer William Gerhardi, Mansfield stressed the need for a distanced objectivity: ". . . you falsify the tone . . . ," she wrote. "[Y]ou . . . tell us what we must feel about [subjects], what the sight of them really meant, and that's not necessary. . . . [T]hey are being 'shown off' rather than seen."[16]

In her own fiction Mansfield's practice was to efface herself from her writing while she merged with the object of which she wrote. She described this "transformed subjectivity"[17] in a letter to Dorothy Brett: "When I pass the apple stalls I cannot help stopping and staring until I feel that I, myself, am changing into an apple, too. . . . When I write about ducks I swear that I am a white duck with a round eye. . . . I don't see how art is going to make that divine *spring* into the bounding outlines of things if it hasn't passed through the process of trying to *become* the things before recreating them" (*Letters,* 1:330)

She wrote Richard Murry of her consciousness of voice, of the sound of her prose: "In *Miss Brill* I choose not only the length of every sentence, but even the sound of every sentence. I choose the rise and fall of every paragraph to fit her, and to fit her on that day at that very moment. After I'd written it I read it aloud—numbers of times—just as one would *play over* a musical composition . . . until it fitted her. . . . there mustn't be one single word out of place, or one word that could be taken out" (Murry, ed., *Letters,* 2:360)

It was possibly a benefit that illness increasingly imposed on her withdrawal from the literary society she disliked. But it also limited the data on which she based her final view of humanity: isolated, with hope of neither human understanding nor supernatural help or pity. Though she gallantly affirmed beauty to the very end, the casual destructive forces always lurked nearby, and in any joy sadness waited. Mansfield's life taught her to admire the rose but, in her own repeated image, to look for "the snail under the leaf."

Perhaps she always instinctively knew and resisted this negation. "The Tiredness of Rosabel," written in 1908 when she began her London career, contains the seeds of many later stories and of the characteristic

Mansfield technique. The story concerns the wish-fulfillment reverie of a girl described as tragically optimistic. From this shopgirl who returns to her drab room, hungry because she bought violets instead of dinner, arises a downward progress of impoverished women who awake, the dreaming over, to angry landladies and dreary choices. Viola of "The Swing of the Pendulum" (1911) flirts with a strange man but recoils at the realism of his intentions. In "Pictures" (1919) the older, defeated Ada Moss, wearing artificial violets, yields at last to prostitution to get the dinner Rosabel could go without. The tragic optimism has run out.

The technique of "The Tiredness of Rosabel" is similarly prophetic of the writing yet to come. It begins in the middle of the situation, which is delineated through the observations of Rosabel as she rides a bus home from work. Antithetic images lead to the antithetic conclusion. Dull, dirty streets are turned to opal and silver, even to Venice, in the view of the wistfully imaginative girl. Human ambivalence appears as she thinks of herself in the very language she had scorned when scanning a romantic novel over another girl's shoulder on the bus. The insolent, suggestive Harry, though he insulted her in the shop, is desirable. Throughout the reverie, while Rosabel sees herself as exotically rich and then married to Harry, her fatigue recurs thematically. Nor is the odor of violets or her longing for dinner forgotten. The story remains within Rosabel's consciousness, flowing smoothly back in time, then forward in reverie, but maintaining awareness always of the present Rosabel, hungry and tired in her drab little room. Only after Rosabel has fallen asleep does the author intrude (unnecessarily, but Mansfield has not yet learned this) for a compassionate summation. In shape and to some extent style, the story is like many Mansfield will compose. Even her last completed story, "The Canary," takes place entirely in the consciousness of a woman who seems to speak first in the present, momentarily of the future, then of the past, and finally, to sum up, in the present again. Nor is there in that last story much alteration of the writer's attitude.

The technique of "The Tiredness of Rosabel" is not striking today, but for 1908 it was an astonishing departure. Mansfield was not only emotionally and physically homeless at that time; she was artistically isolated. It is not known whether she had yet read any Chekhov. No departures from English storytelling traditions informed or supported her exploration of the craft. James Joyce had finished all but three stories of *Dubliners* in 1905, but he could not get the book published until 1914.[18] Virginia Woolf published no novels before 1915 and no stories before 1917, but when her stories did appear, they were very much in the

Mansfield manner, marked by the same personal immediacy of view, the same acute perception of detail. In summer 1917 as their friendship began, Mansfield wrote Woolf of the likeness: ". . . We have got the same job, Virginia, and it is really very curious and thrilling that we should both . . . be after so very nearly the same thing. We are, you know: there's no denying it" (*Letters*, 1:327).

If in 1908 Mansfield had read Conrad, Stephen Crane, E. M. Forster, Bennett, or Galsworthy (to name a few contemporary writers of reputation), she found in them traditional form. The older style of story, from which she departed immediately, relied heavily on a plot in which "something happened": a significant change in the situation, with stress on a climax and a conclusion. In "The Tiredness of Rosabel" there is no change and very little action. The author, despite her final intrusion, relies upon the reader to make the inferences necessary to understand the emotional suggestions of her story. It is a static episode, very free in its substitution of emotional for chronological order. Though not baldly so, the intended effect is painful, an effect of caustic pathos. The reader is expected to recognize that, though there is sympathy for the sleeping Rosabel, there is mockery, a subtle feminist rejection, implicit in the account of her daydream compounded of "romantic" novels and acceptance of her traditional gender role.

The story is distinctly modern, so far in advance of many of those to appear in *In a German Pension* that one wonders whether the editorial policy of the *New Age*, Mansfield's first London publisher, interfered in these stories with an artistic development which had to rely more heavily on the intelligence and sensitivity of the reader than editors striving for popular circulation are usually willing to do. For about five years the taste and probably the environments of the *New Age* and of *Rhythm* retarded Mansfield's experimentation. Only toward the end of 1913, when she lacked a ready publisher, did she begin to find her way back to and to go beyond the achievement of "Rosabel."

Chapter Two

In a German Pension and the *New Age*

Katherine Mansfield's first professional publication in England, "The Child-Who-Was-Tired," is so nearly like Chekhov's "Spat Khochetsia" that the question of plagiarism has often been argued.[1] An early, reasonable view is that of Ronald Sutherland, who finds in the parallels between the two stories no plagiarism or imitation "save the commonplace appropriation of a thematic idea and plot detail from the storehouse of existing literature." Sutherland, indeed, though he acknowledges probable borrowing of ideas in four instances—this one, "Marriage à la Mode," "Taking the Veil," and "The Fly"—concludes that in each case Mansfield "produced a story characteristic of herself and entirely foreign to Anton Chekhov" and that Chekhov "in no significant way influenced" her writing.[2] With time critical approaches change. Kaplan (202), arguing recently from a feminist point of view, calls the story Mansfield's "attempt to deconstruct a phallocentric myth by retelling it."

Certainly Mansfield found in Chekhov approaches congenial to her own developing literary impulse, and in borrowing his materials she altered them enough to make them her own. Though she would never "play the sedulous ape," the discovery of a kindred feeling and intention in short story form was undoubtedly encouraging. In her highly individual way, and as inexplicably, her literary development parallels in broad outline Chekhov's move from immature caricatures and comic anecdotes written swiftly for daily and weekly papers to short stories which are the foundation of the contemporary tradition in fiction.

The German translation "Schlafen" is found in volume 4 of the Chekhov *Gesammelte Werke,* but perhaps more influential for the author of *In a German Pension* is volume 1, which contains "Humorische Geschichte."[3] Here Mansfield would have found the "vaudeville element," which Renata Pogglioli calls "a lasting, or . . . recurring, ingredient in [Chekhov's] narrative work."[4] The pension stories are to a large extent results of Mansfield's Bavarian experience, but such pieces as

"The Baron," "The Sister of the Baroness," "Frau Fischer," and "The Modern Soul," with their obvious yet dryly comic final illuminations, take on the shape and tone of Chekhov's pre-1886 journalism. As with Chekhov, the introduction of compassion to the characterization of later stories adds a moral dimension which changes the humor to an irony not always amusing. Depth has increased immeasurably between the last sentence of "A Birthday" and the last sentence of "The Fly," but the anecdotal patterning defined by those final words is the same.

Katherine Mansfield is often credited with reinforcing Chekhov's influence on English writing. But it was an already created admiration of his manner which resulted in the acceptance of her work by the *New Age*. In 1909 Arnold Bennett, under the guise of "Jacob Tonson," had praised the Russian highly in that very periodical. His remarks were the culmination of a taste that had been developing since the first Chekhov translations had begun to appear in the 1890s. The translation of 13 volumes of his short stories by Constance Garnett between 1916 and 1922 probably did more to influence the development of English fiction in *his* manner than the few slender Mansfield volumes did.

Moreover, in 1910, when the *New Age* began enthusiastically to publish almost all the prose Mansfield wrote for two years,[5] she pleased with more than her resemblance to Chekhov. Literary criticism was in the hands of A. E. Randall, who, Paul Selver remembers, specialized in "scathing wit" and based his "caustic effectiveness on a rather scanty stock of ideas." Trevor Allen favored the weekly with "sulphuric parodies," victimizing "the sillier poetasters of the time." T. E. Hulme provided, besides philosophy, anti-German bias.[6] The mood of the publication clearly welcomed, therefore, the sort of stories that made up Katherine Mansfield's first book, of which she wrote to John Middleton Murry 10 years later: "I cannot have the German Pension republished under any circumstances. It is far too *immature* & I don't even acknowledge it today. I mean I don't 'hold' by it. I cant go foisting that kind of stuff on the public—*it's not good enough.* . . . Its positively juvenile, and besides its not what I mean: its a lie" (*Letters*, 3:206).[7]

What became a "lie" to the author of "Prelude" was probably exactly what had won her acceptance in the *New Age*: the caustic lack of compassion and the emotional and intellectual limitations so frequently but undeliberately exposed in the complacent protagonist, clearly the persona of the Katherine Mansfield of 1910. The technical inadequacy must also have chagrined a writer as sternly critical of her work as the later Mansfield had become. Some of the sketches of Germans living in pen-

sions read like what they no doubt were: the slightly touched-up journal
of an embittered, defensive colonial girl who has mistaken her provincial
literary success for sophistication.

The stories did not appear regularly in the *New Age*. There were four
periods of literary output separated by periods of silence. These gaps
indicate either that some of the stories were not written in Bavaria or
that they demanded considerable rewriting after Mansfield began to
publish. Later she wrote gratefully to the editor, A. R. Orage, "You
taught me how to write." (Alpers, 325) It may be possible to detect the
nature of his instructions by examining her work in four segments.

Between 24 February and 24 March 1910 appeared "The Child-
Who-Was-Tired," "Germans at Meat," "The Baron," and "The Luft
Bad." In the July and August issues there were four more: "At
Lehmann's," "Frau Brechenmacher Attends a Wedding," "The Sister of
the Baroness," and "Frau Fischer." After an eight-month absence, consis-
tent publication resumed in May 1911. By September five stories and an
uncollected sketch were printed. The stories were "A Birthday," "The
Modern Soul," "The Breidenbach Family in England," "The Journey to
Bruges," and "Being a Truthful Adventure." The last three, dated 1910
by Murry, were not collected in *In a German Pension*. The volume did,
however, include "The Swing of the Pendulum," "A Blaze," and "The
Advanced Lady," none of which had been published before.

Of the first group, "The Child-Who-Was-Tired" stands apart, having no
connection with the pension scene of the other stories. The longing of
the child for annihilation is thematically suggested by her repeated doz-
ing into or attempting to tell the dream of "a little white road that led to
nowhere, and where nobody walked at all."[8] The story begins in this
dream and moves through a day of longing for the "little white road";
then, as the observations of the child grow more and more fatigued and
hallucinatory—people are alternately giants and dolls—and the conversation of the adults indicates that she is a half-wit, the child has her
"beautiful marvellous idea" (98). Laughing and clapping her hands, she
suffocates the baby and at last escapes into her dream. The lack of reality in the major part of the child's day and expectations is enhanced by
the abstract designations of the main characters: the Man, the Frau, the
Child-Who-Was-Tired. In contrast to these are the children with real
names—Anton, Hans, and Lena—who quarrel viciously and are dressed,
fed, and beaten before disappearing to school. The tasks of the day—the
potatoes, the laundry, the baby—which burden the child, the grass in

the meadow, the people on the real road down which she longs to escape to the dreamed-of road—all are solidly perceived. Thus a rhythm of alternately focused reality and unfocused hallucination is achieved.

The narrative is flawed only by a few failures in diction, which break momentarily the illusion of the child's viewpoint. But the lapse is brief, and the story is otherwise well built and conveys a strong impression.

Of course, Mansfield had read Chekhov's story. The plots of "Sleepy" and "The-Child-Who-Was-Tired" are the same. But by locating the consciousness through which the story is told in the Child's mind, Mansfield increases specificity and considerably changes tone and meaning. Though grimmer, the Child's position is akin to that of the earlier Rosabel, exploited in the workplace and by her economically assigned position in society.

Mansfield could have read "Sleepy" at Queen's College as early as 1903, when it was included in R. E. C. Long's translation, *The Black Monk*,[9] and her literary curiosity was expanding. The book was acquired in 1904 by the General Assembly Library at Wellington, where she read during her 1907–08 return to New Zealand (Meyers, 25). As her later recurring motif of the abused child suggests, such a story would have become embedded in her consciousness whenever she read it. Did she tell herself on first reading, "Varka is a stick figure. I can do better"? Or did the plot become a hazy memory, inaccurately recalled, possibly even haunting her dreams? For the image of the "little white road that led to nowhere" expressed a significance central to Mansfield's ambivalent perception of life.

If she read the story for the first time (or again) in German, distanced by the Germanic typography—black letter type with all the nouns capitalized—and, of course, the language itself, it would have seemed doubly abstract, another stimulus to challenge Chekhov's version.

The formal alterations, especially the telling totally as envisioned by the Child, suggest that the impact of the story had been long internalized, rather than a deliberate, immediate revision. All of Chekhov's exposition is gone: the flashback to the death of Varka's father, her mother's begging, and her delivery into servitude for survival. Mansfield accounts for her economically, toward the end of the day, in the Frau's two gossipy sentences: "She's the free-born one—daughter of the waitress at the railway station. They found her mother trying to squeeze her head in the wash-hand jug, and the child's half silly" (97).

The story begins where it ends, in the Child's dream of "walking along the little white road." As the refrain repeats, it becomes clear that the Child yearns not only for sleep but to escape down the road she dreamed of. Her days and nights are crowded with chores, commands, abusive adults, and children she must serve. The Child desires isolation, to get away from all that makes her life wretched. The theme of longing is repeated twice at the beginning, as she tells herself a wish-fulfillment fairy tale that melts into a vague recollection of a child who played all day in a meadow and wasn't tired (96). When happy people walk past in warm sunshine, the child thinks that if she could follow, could walk far enough, she might come to the little white road (97). Unlike Chekhov's dark, muddy road peopled by men and shadows, the white road is pleasant, desirable.

Mansfield increases the Child's burdens by the addition of three badly behaved children, whose need of discipline increases the abuse of the Child. Her horror and motivation are intensified by the expectation of another baby. Yet Mansfield typically introduces that information as a muted joke of wordplay that results in misunderstanding. After the Child has tried to excuse the baby's crying by explaining that he is teething, the Man says, "There's another one coming." The Child thinks he means another tooth and feels for it in the baby's mouth (93). This momentary bit of woman's realism, by lightening the mood, intensifies, for the reader, the subsequent despair and terror which motivate the exhausted Child's final solution.

Is this anything like Chekhov's unremittingly gloomy tale? Abstractly he drives home Varka's position, with less abuse and fewer burdens, relying on an omniscient author's stentorian, doomsday rhetoric: ". . . in her semi-slumber she cannot understand the force that binds her, hand and foot, and crushes her, and ruins her life. She . . . seeks that force that she may rid herself of it. But she cannot find it." Then, as she hears the baby cry,

> she finds the enemy that is crushing her heart.
> The enemy is the child. (Chekhov, 187)

Mansfield specifies the labor and cruelty perversely complacent adults can "righteously" visit upon a helpless female child.[10] Chekhov's abstract "force" is absurdly reduced to a crying baby.

Not at all convincing. I can imagine a wise young Mansfield wondering, on first reading, whether "silly" Varka would have understood had the child been completely awake. Or perhaps more wisely still, Mansfield had forgotten this passage when, a few years later, she composed with a more sensitive vision.

Mansfield compels the reader to see a real child fastening her petti-
coat strings, chipping up kindling to light the fire, selecting potatoes
with big eyes because they are easier to peel, from fatigue accurately
feeling pains in head and neck, hallucinating as one does after days without sleep. The Child has a woman's knowledge of clothing, housework,
and the care of babies. She even knows where to find a bolster with
which to smother the baby, who realistically struggles like a duck with
its head off (another image Mansfield will repeat at a peak of horror in
"At the Bay"). Compared with all this felt, homely detail, Dr. Chekhov
appears remote from his material. He has not entered into the emotion,
which Mansfield deploys in her scenes, to overwhelm the wretched
Child.

Clearly "The Child-Who-Was-Tired" is not plagiarized. The story
recalls techniques used to describe that other very tired Rosabel. Both
the Child and Rosabel dwell within a consciousness that alternates
between reality and a dream world. There is no more need to acknowledge Chekhov as a source than Shakespeare needed to advertise his intertextuality.[11]

But one more consideration remains. What reason is there to assume
that Mansfield didn't tell Orage that her story was an improvement on
Chekhov, a writer well known to the editor of the New Age? And perhaps Orage, assuming that his iconoclastic readers would recognize the
Chekhovian origin and applaud the new version, didn't bother to mention the obvious.

The discussion of plagiarism, which began as a scholarly note in 1935
and crescendoed as irrelevant but thematic character assassination in a
biography of 1988, has persisted too long as a cause célèbre of careerist
discussion. For more than a half-century Mansfield has been unnecessarily condemned or defended by eager Quellenforschunger. Would that it
were not too much to hope that my detailed comparisons will render the
topic no longer obligatory.

The tone of the first three German pieces (despite "the Frau," "The
Child-Who-Was-Tired" is not particularly German) is quite different; it
sardonically mocks the behavior of people living in a boardinghouse and
taking "the cure." Like future stories, these begin in the middle of the
action, taking it for granted that the reader will soon understand the setting. The characters still have abstract names, because they represent
types, not individuals. The stories are almost entirely dialogue, inter-
spersed with detailed descriptions of the boarders, their gestures, and

unfortunately, the overstated reactions of the first-person narrator. The plots are essentially jokes. The effect is comical but it is caricature.

The most successful, as the most genuinely amusing, is "Germans at Meat." In this story, which became the first one of *In a German Pension,* the antagonism between Germany and England is immediately brought to light. The English girl narrator is implicitly attacked (as the representative of her nation) for huge breakfasts, small families, bad tea, and fear of a German invasion. Her observations of the enormous quantity of food consumed at the German table, of the preoccupation with internal physical processes (which she prudishly wards off by clever vaudeville-style interruptions), and of the grotesquely misinformed chauvinism would provide her with a subtle victory. But she spoils the satire by her intrusive, defensive comments: "I felt I was bearing the burden of the nation's preposterous breakfast—I who drank a cup of coffee while buttoning my blouse in the morning" (37) and "He fixed his cold blue eyes upon me with an expression which suggested a thousand premeditated invasions" (38), when Herr Rat (the name must have been chosen with delight) challenges her teamaking ability. After Fraulein Steigelauer says the doctor has advised fruit for her health, "she very obviously followed the advice" (39). Even worse is the girl's overt challenge, for she must stoutly announce for England, "We certainly do not want Germany" (40). The comedic exposure of crudity seems overdone when Herr Hoffman, moved by his enjoyable sweating, "wiped his neck and face with his dinner napkin and carefully cleaned his ears" (39). Surely this is humor on the Laurel and Hardy or English music hall level.

The opening of "The Baron" involves two self-conscious observations and one sardonic remark (not understood by the dense German woman addressed) by the English girl, before it shifts momentarily to implied humor: the Frau Oberregierungsrat laments, "My omelette is empty— *empty,* and this is the third I have tried" (41). Excessive comment and exaggeration continue to dissipate what could have been clever intimations. When the pension manager obsequiously presents the Baron his mail on a tray, the English girl feels "disappointed that there was not a salute of twenty-five guns" (42).

The subject mocked is snobbery, as the pensioners speculate about and admire the aloof habits of their silent Baron. The English girl must to some extent share that snobbery, since her wish-fulfillment victory this time consists of their wonder when she comes home under the Baron's umbrella. Though she mocks, she is as curious as the rest; so surely she too is deflated upon learning that his interesting habits reflect distrust of the servants and his greedy desire for double portions of food. Her ironic ending belongs to the schoolgirl: "Sic transit gloria German mundi" (44). In fact, she found it in her adolescent reading of Marie Bashkirtself.[12]

"The Luft Bad," if the first sentence were in the past tense so as to emphasize the change of attitude in the ending, would have the technical balance of "The Child-Who-Was-Tired." It consists almost entirely of banal conversation and the progressive withdrawal of the narrator from Hungarians and Russians as well as Germans. The subject is a sardonic change of attitude. In one day the value of an umbrella is learned: it helps one to avoid the conversation of one's fellow sunbathers. The repeated themes of self-consciousness about her bare legs and speculation about umbrellas unify this tightly built but trivial story.

"The Luft Bad," though slight, marks a new approach in Mansfield's work: the protagonist moves through a tenuous chain of experiences and undergoes a minute development of awareness. Essentially the substance of one type of Chekhov story, it also becomes part of the Mansfield stock-in-trade. She explores this structure in her July stories, "At Lehmann's" and "Frau Brechenmacher Attends a Wedding." But for August she has surely reverted to the superficialities of her Bavarian journal. If the *New Age* editor had observed her shift in manner, he did not apparently encourage it.

"At Lehmann's" unfolds the sexual awakening of an innocent young hotel waitress, Sabina. Contrapuntally, as the "the Young Man" customer in two visits arouses her animal instincts, Frau Lehmann, swollen and unappetizing, suffers in labor. The ignorant girl knows that to have a baby requires a husband, but she does not know why. When she first feels drawn to the Young Man she is immediately aware of Frau Lehmann's footsteps. This rhythmic alternation of emphasis, first used in "The Child-Who-Was-Tired," defines the form of the story. "Ugly— ugly—ugly," Sabina mutters, returning from an errand for the self-pitying Frau to the Young Man. That night in bed, made aware of her body by the Young Man's picture of a nude woman, she longs for a mirror and hugs her body, immediately thinking, "I wouldn't be the Frau for one hundred marks" (76).

All the next day Sabina's work in the café is accompanied by the groans of the woman in labor, gradually confirming the girl's rejection of such experience: "I will not hear it. No, it is too much." With the Young Man's return, she feels happy again. So the seesaw of feeling continues.

She is frightened but does not reject his kiss in the cloakroom. Then, as he embraces her, there is a "frightful, tearing shriek" (78), and Sabina, hearing the cry of a baby, shrieks too and rushes from the room in a final revulsion.

The more ambitious "Frau Brechenmacher Attends a Wedding" is, in several respects, like "At Lehmann's." Both stories open with a short sentence that begins the action and locates the point of view within the consciousness of the main character. (Almost immediately in the former, as though the writer were practicing already for the virtuosity of "The Daughters of the Late Colonel," there is a successfully handled, brief shift of viewpoint to the child Rosa, a shift which unfortunately serves no function within the story's form, but recalls the abused child motif.) Frau Brechenmacher, mother of five, would also like to avoid sexual relations, but her husband, recalling with amusement her innocence and resistance on their wedding night, is unaware of her reluctance. Here is the first Mansfield characterization of the self-centered, crude family man whose overwhelming sexuality drains the life of his women. He will shortly be further defined as Andreas Binzer, will evolve through a long line of prototypes to Stanley Burnell, and will end in a final denunciation as the self-pitying boss of "The Fly."

The full scene necessary for the wedding in "Frau Brechenmacher" demands an extended technical effort. On the way to the wedding Mansfield abandons her limited viewpoint for comments more in the style of her favorite pensioner. She cannot resist denouncing in her own voice first the landlord of the Gasthaus, who bullies the waitresses, and then Herr Brechenmacher himself. Control and the Frau's viewpoint are regained as she listens to the guest's spiteful and gossipy conversation, reminiscent again of the German boardinghouse. Her feelings fluctuate, but sometimes the material is so raggedly controlled that the author seems to have forgotten where her sympathies lie: surprising non sequiturs appear.

But essentially Frau Brechenmacher responds to her environment like Mansfield's pension persona. She sympathizes with the reluctant, uneasy bride. When her husband presents the newlyweds with the group's present, a silver coffeepot which is opened to reveal the usual comment about having children, the bride screams. The groom is amused and exposes the joke to the laughing guests. But Frau Brechenmacher feels herself derided and laughed at (61). This response and her image of the bride as "an iced cake all ready to be cut and served in neat little pieces to the bridegroom beside her" (58) prepare the reader for her climactic

gesture of pained withdrawal. Walking home and preparing supper, the
Frau has asked herself repeatedly the unanswerable question, "What is it
all for?" Before going to bed she concludes, "Always the same . . . how
stupid." Then, as she lies in bed and her drunken husband lurches forward, "she put her arm across her face like a child who expected to be
hurt" (62).

This closing penetrates the mask of Katherine Mansfield. The tone
agrees with that of her journal entry of June 1909, probably written in
Bavaria.[13] There, after recording her pain, cold, and confusion of body,
she longs for the comfort of childhood: "The only adorable thing I can
imagine is for my Grandmother to put me to bed and bring me a bowl
of hot bread and milk, and . . . say . . . : 'There, darling, isn't that nice?'
Oh, what a miracle of happiness that would be" (*Journal,* 42). Her latent,
wistful image of herself as an abandoned, comfortless child accounts for
her sensitive preoccupation in so many early stories with overworked or
otherwise mistreated children: Rosa, the daughter of Frau
Brechenmacher, who in her determined, secret mind is kin to Helen of
"New Dresses"; Pearl Button; "The Little Girl"; "The Child-Who-Was-
Tired"; and the child of "The Woman at the Store." Gradually these children must grow up into innocent but still tired, overworked, somehow
menaced young girls like Sabina and later "The Little Governess" or the
innocent of "Something Childish."[14] Mansfield's poetry of that time is
also full of children, but the poems were not offered to the callous *New
Age,* and the mask is secure again in the stories published in August.

"The Sister of the Baroness" is a companion piece to "The Baron,"
paralleling it in both theme and amateurish technique. The subject is
again snobbery, but this time the Germans spend their admiration not
on a greedy nobleman but on a masquerading young girl, the daughter
of a dressmaker. Where in the earlier story only the narrator learned of
the clay feet, in this story all are disabused in an ending as swift as that
of "At Lehmann's." But this ending is followed by an anticlimactic summary statement like that of "The Baron": "Tableau grandissimo!" (49)—
again very schoolgirlish.

Meanwhile the narrator has once more overdone the caricature and
overasserted her contempt for German aristocracy and romanticism. A
poet's tie lies in his coffee while he stares soulfully at the noble ladies.
The narrator thinks, "Death spasms of his Odes to Solitude!" Of his
poem to the young girl, the narrator says: "Nine verses equally lovely
commanded her to equally violent action. . . . had she followed his
advice not even the remainder of her life in a convent would have given

her time to recover her breath." On the typical German student a final aphorism is framed: "He had hitherto relied upon three scars and a ribbon to produce an effect" (47). Gossip, snobbery, and greed are all challenged in one efficient breakfast image: "Anecdotes of the High Born were poured out, sweetened, and sipped: we gorged on scandals of High Birth generously buttered" (45). And romance is disposed of when the German student whispers, "How I should adore to kiss you. But you know I am suffering from severe nasal catarrh." This admission is enough, but the narrator hears more: "Sixteen times last night did I count myself sneezing." The eavesdropper expresses her feeling by throwing her volume of Mörike's romantic lyrics into the lilac bush (49).

In "Frau Fischer," as in "The Luft Bad," the narrator rejects German society, this time in the shape of aggressive advances by a widow who warns her, "When I meet new people I squeeze them dry" (54). The narrator thinks of wisecracks and self-consciously congratulates herself on her forbearance in not making them, but, of course, the reader has benefited, though the Germans have not. The music hall comic's trick of contrasting banal, practical conversation with lofty literature is employed, as excerpts from the "Miracles of Lourdes" are interrupted by details of preparation of the rooms Frau Fischer has engaged, until "[n]ot even the white roses upon the feet of the Virgin could flourish in that atmosphere" (51).[15] An almost Gogolesque comedy appears in the phrasing of Herr Rat's Mack Sennett–like adventure in Turkey "with a drunken guide who was bitten by a mad dog and fell over a precipice into a field of attar of roses" (53).

The impossibility of English-German rapport is analyzed by Frau Fischer: "You do not seem to enjoy discussing the functions of the body. . . . How can we hope to understand anybody, knowing nothing of their stomachs?" (52). So by implication one of the major protests of *In a German Pension* is inversely crystallized. In this story the narrator also argues more insistently than usual about waiters and marital relations and is finally goaded into asserting, "I consider child-bearing the most ignominious of all professions" (55).[16]

The technical unity of the sketch is effected by the word *squeeze*. The squeezing promised by Frau Fischer has failed consistently. The last sentence, then, is obviously clever: "She squeezed my hand, but I didn't squeeze back" (56).

After a lapse of eight months, broken only by the December appearance of "A Fairy Story" in *The Open Window,* Mansfield's work again began to appear in the *New Age*. Of the five stories printed between May and September 1911, only two, "A Birthday" and "A Modern Soul," were collected for *In a German Pension*.[17] Only "A Birthday" suggests that Mansfield is developing as a writer. The others are in the manner of her usual *New Age* pieces.

In a fashion, "A Birthday" takes up, again "offstage," the action of "At Lehmann's": a woman is in painful labor during the time of the story and finally gives birth to a child. A young maid is present, again innocently curious and finally, loathing men, vows herself to sterility. These attitudes are akin to the sentiments of Sabina; this time they are asserted, however, with a comic effect that is out of keeping with the tone and intention of the story, which is, in fact, focused on Andreas Binzer.

The dissection of the man who is sensitive only to his own sensitivity is Mansfield's purpose, and as in many later instances, she realizes that the knife is best wielded by the individual who deserves it. Unerringly the details of Binzer's day assail his self-pitying nerves, to damn him in the reader's eyes by the time his son is born. He takes it as a matter of course that his wife will climb a rickety ladder on which he does not care to trust himself. He makes no connection between her loss of youth since their marriage and her having borne three children, as the doctor reminds him. He regrets that he has gone out without breakfast to get this doctor for his wife, and he is in many ways annoyed by the man's competent, realistic conversation. The maid too makes him fear for his health when she spits on his shoe before shining it, and she nearly ruins his hearty breakfast by not appearing promptly with a warm plate for the fish. It is annoying also that his Sunday must be spoiled by the absence of the children and by the inattentiveness of his wife on this occasion. And the wind, that New Zealand wind[18] which will rise to similar effect again in "The Wind Blows," unnerves him further.

But this is not caricature. There is tenderness too in Andreas Binzer; it is aroused by the sound of church bells and by resulting memories of other Sunday mornings with his wife. He looks at and even kisses her photograph. At that moment her cry is heard and, like Sabina's in "At Lehmann's," his feeling changes. Her photographic smile oppresses him and he comes close to destroying the picture. This sequence, as well as his previous meditation about developing his business for the boy whose birth he awaits, clearly foreshadows "The Fly." The interlude has displayed a new depth of perception in the author, but no lack of conviction about the dominant nature of Binzer. His moment of terror—when the wind dies and the house is suddenly silent—he would express in the self-pitying, sentimental words, "My beloved wife has passed away!" Instead he learns that the son has indeed been born. He triumphantly sums up his day in words which foreshadow the self-congratulations of Raoul Duquette: "Nobody can accuse *me* of not knowing what suffering is" (91). It is a fitting conclusion from Mansfield's first fallible narrator.

The other three stories are marked by the flaws of her earliest attempts with the pension guests. The same excessively sardonic narrator caricatures too much. The comedy is often slapstick—what better subject than German boarders giving a benefit performance for afflicted infants, as in "The Modern Soul"? But "The Journey to Bruges" and "A Truthful Adventure" have abandoned the Germans to express a more general contempt for humanity. In the latter the narrator, shamelessly identified now as "Katherine," is opposed to everything which crosses her path. Ladies, servants, painters, boatmen, an old school friend from New Zealand, guidebooks, and women's suffrage, even Bruges itself, shrivel before her disaffected eye.

In March of the following year two more Mansfield pieces appeared, so poor that neither she nor even Murry ever cared to reprint them. In two years, of the 16 stories and sketches Mansfield wrote for the *New Age,* only four exhibit the degree of control and perception that forecast work of literary value. The others display only the sort of competence with witty phrase and situation that might today sustain, for a season, a second-rate comedy series for television. Apparently, despite her grateful letter to Orage in later years, the taste of the *New Age* was not demanding; its influence was not, therefore, destined to elicit excellence from Katherine Mansfield.

The form of these earlier stories is sometimes flawed, but what is the purpose, what is the mode of the fledging writer? Of course, the Germans are mocked for their gross appetites, their narcissistic interest in their digestive organs, and even more for their smug, nationalistic self-esteem—a people so humorless and egotistically obtuse that they fail to recognize the narrator's mockery. Out of this blindness rises much of the comedy of the pension stories, which are, read correctly, very funny.

Leonard Woolf delighted in Mansfield's humor. "When we first knew her, she was extraordinarily amusing," he recalled. "I don't think anyone has ever made me laugh more than she did in those days. She would . . . tell at immense length a kind of saga, of her experiences as an actress or of how and why Koteliansky howled like a dog. . . . There was not the shadow of a gleam of a smile on her mask of a face, and the extraordinary funniness of the story was enhanced by the flashes of her astringent wit. . . . She was a very serious writer, but her gifts were those of an intense realist, with a superb sense of ironic humour and fundamental cynicism."[19] He is describing a deadpan comic performer, a professional role during Mansfield's early days in London, when she was sometimes hired to entertain at parties and also appeared at the Cave of the Golden Calf nightclub (Alpers, 105–6; Meyers, 37; Tomalin, 60).

Description of comedy rarely replicates its effect. To find the laughter in Mansfield's youthful wit, the reader must hear it, aloud or mentally, as live performance, the stand-up comedy of nightclub entertainment. The pension stories consist almost entirely of dialogue. The narrator's scornful, deflating remarks are one-liners. The Germans, by creating contexts for the narrator's derision, act as her straightmen and -women. If the stories are flawed, it is because the comic dialogue ceases when the narrator speaks not as an unwilling, sardonic participant in an alien culture but, unnecessarily, to hammer home her views, to underline her contempt or dismay.

But as Woolf noted, Mansfield was a serious writer. Subtly, patterns of behavior and emphasis convey a social and political source of her disapproval. The pun of Herr Rat may be obvious. More knowledge of German reveals that the few male guests are named by their occupations or have names with derisive associations: "Herr Windberg and his trombone" is immediately evident; there are also *Langen* (reach), *Lehmann* (vassal), *Hoffman* (courtier or hoping man), *Brechenmacher* (the base *brech* can mean vomit, emetic, diarrhea). This derogation might be attributed to the historical peculiarities of German nomenclature,[20] were it not for the naming of the women.

The few unmarried women possess derogatory names: *Fraulein Winkel* (humble condition) and *Fraulein Stiegelauer* (stair-lurker, spy). But the dominant guest population consists of married women, almost invariably named only by the occupations of their husbands: *Frauen Oberlehrer* (senior teacher), *Kellermann* (tavernkeeper, waiter), *Ledermann* (leatherman), *Oberregierungsrat* (senior government councillor). The loss of feminine identity rises to the extreme of *Frau Feldleutnantswitwe,* a military widow who foreshadows the daughters of the late colonel in her inability to escape her dead. In one of the earliest stories, "The Baron," the married women talk about the underwear of their husbands, the unmarried women about the outer clothing of "Possible Ones" (43).

Beginning with this very accurate observation of a nation which deprives married women of their own personal names and focuses their conversation on the presence or pursuit of the marital tie, Mansfield's feminist subversion continues in "The Modern Soul" with her amused, surreal description of married women at an evening party: "dressed like upholstered chairs" and the unmarried, "like draped muslin dressing-table covers" (67). The realistic observer renders as absurd the position of women considered appropriate among the German bourgeoisie.

The narrator is cagey about her own identity.[21] Though in the *New Age* version of "Germans at Meat" she is "Kathleen" and "the English woman," the change to first person in *In a German Pension* (37) allows her to declare that she is not American and "hardly English," provoking a display of German ignorance in the assertion that she must be one or the other (81).[22] But she "acknowledges" that she is English in "The Advanced Lady" (101).

The narrator is no longer Kathleen, and since she denounces child-bearing but will not describe the ailment which has brought her to the spa, she is apparently not visibly pregnant (52, 55). She mocks the assumption of her acceptability as a married woman by creating a sea captain husband, her "virgin conception," and by revealing to the reader her plan to drown him off Cape Horn. Though "imperfectly disassociated from her creator" (Dunbar, 2), the narrator is not Mansfield but a character through whom she can deconstruct, as the nonpension stories clearly show, not only German attitudes but those of the conservative New Zealand society she has escaped.

Three more stories, not published before, appeared in *In a German Pension*. "The Advanced Lady," which takes place in the pension, is in the manner of the other stories set there, but "The Swing of the Pendulum" and "A Blaze" strike a new note. If the women of the German boarding-house have flirted, they have done so decorously. These two stories, though a slight attempt is made in the names of the characters to relate them to a German scene, suggest instead experiments at living in an English bohemia. In both a woman toys briefly with the affections of a man, recoils, and returns to an earlier male tie.

Viola of "The Swing of the Pendulum" is an innocent girl, who day-dreams like Rosabel; battles her surprising wooer, though with greater vigor, as "The Little Governess" will; and foreshadows in several respects Ada Moss of "Pictures." Viola's swing of feeling from the apparently faithful though poverty-stricken lover, Casimir, to the well-to-do, idle, sensual stranger, and back from the aggressive attentions of the stranger to Casimir, belongs entirely to an unreal world. Even her room is dingy poverty one moment, the lair of a great courtesan the next. It is the older, defeated artist, Miss Moss, who is really compelled to confront in the more mature story the solution to poverty that youthful Viola merely toys with.

In "A Blaze" Elsa, catlike in her desire for admiration, causes the "blaze" quite knowingly, but she is equally withdrawn from the dangers of her flirtation. Almost entirely in dialogue, the story is one of the few which makes no use of a viewpoint character. The only hint of the author's meaning rests in the ironies implicit in the somewhat deceived husband's final appraisal: "God! What a woman you are" (124).

The stories collected for *In a German Pension*—published in December 1911—announce themes and techniques which were to become permanent characteristics of Mansfield's writing. Though she has not yet identified the scene, she has begun to exploit her New Zealand materials. Her focus is entirely personal, but she is developing from sardonic, bitter rejection toward the mingling of compassion with criticism. Already ill health has begun her years of isolated subjugation to strangers in foreign boardinghouses and hotels; she will never cease to reject these people— with violence in her correspondence, with mounting restraint in her stories. Her exploration of sexual relationships is bluntly begun, but it will become more penetrating, yet more tentative, as she matures. She has already introduced most of her characters: mistreated children; innocent but exploring young girls; garrulous, overbearing single or widowed women; downtrodden, physically wasted wives; and overbearing, self-satisfied husbands. No story has yet focused on a young man, though such an abstract figure provides a sounding board for the experimental young woman of "A Blaze" and waits in the wings, motivating "The Swing of the Pendulum."

Technically, Mansfield has found but perhaps not recognized the form which will best convey her experience. Her stories already begin with little or no introduction of character or scene, usually in the mind of a central figure. She has found a fallible narrator only once, in Andreas Binzer. The physical action, if any (it may be taking place upstairs, offstage), consists of blows to the sensibility. In the weaker German pension stories, this sensibility is static; it merely announces the author's repugnance. The excessively caustic caricatures reflect her immaturity. The stories, however, have technical balance.

In those few stories which promise the future Katherine Mansfield, the purpose is discovery: a shift in awareness, an enlargement of self-knowledge, or, more subtly, an available self-knowledge, rejected by the central character but known by the author and the reader who have followed the progress of this developing consciousness. The irony of such observations is mellowed and strengthened as the young writer learns not to state her conclusion overtly.

Though *In a German Pension* was enthusiastically reviewed (Alpers, 129), Mansfield was nearly finished, for a time, with writing for the *New Age,* which had spawned 10 of the stories.

Chapter Three
Three Little Magazines

In December 1911 Katherine Mansfield received an encouraging rejection slip from John Middleton Murry, the young editor of a new publication, *Rhythm*. She had sent him a "fairy tale," but the aim of *Rhythm*, announced in the first number, was to reject aestheticism and its limited, if exquisite, vision. Instead the editors cried for "an art that strikes deeper . . . drawing its inspiration from aversion, to a deeper and a broader field . . . in its pity and its brutality it shall be real." Mansfield immediately provided what was required in "The Woman at the Store," and Murry hailed it as "by far the best story that had been sent to *Rhythm*."[1]

For the scene of this story Mansfield drew on her memories of the New Zealand backcountry. The frontier store and the hot, raw, isolated countryside are described in painstaking detail. Dialect is imitated in the speech of the characters, and several of the words employed—*whare, wideawake, milkbilly, sundowners*—need glossing. With this naturalistic technique is blended the brutal subject of murder and insanity.

The story is carefully plotted but departs from what was then traditional form.[2] The opening appearance of the woman carrying a rifle neatly foreshadows the child's drawing, which reveals the murder. Jo's casual, drunken remark, "No use cryin' over spilt 'usbands!" provides irony, as does the woman's deceptive "if I was a secret woman I'd place any confidence in your 'ands" (132). The repeated question concerning the husband's whereabouts and the child's threat to draw a forbidden picture lead easily to the denouement. Mansfield lends emotional weight to the discovery indirectly, through the behavior of her observing characters. Despite the long, exhausting day's ride, the narrator and Jim sit up all night looking at the drawing.

By letting the narrator-participant avoid defining comment, Mansfield presents the reader with a choice of responses: shall it be horror, pity, complicity? With this lack of evaluative closure, the writer has increased the realistic tone. She does remark, however, upon observing the woman, her child, and the store, "Good Lord, what a life!" A trace of the supercilious German pension style intrudes while the narrator is drinking with Jo and the woman: "He reached his hand across the table and held hers, and though the position looked most uncomfortable when they wanted to pass the water and whisky, their hands stuck together as though glued" (132).

It is the effect of isolation and a hard life on the woman that interests Mansfield, rather than the plot of detection. In a central passage the woman utters sentiments akin to those of Frau Brechenmacher; speaking of past conversations with her husband, she says, "Over and over I tells 'im—you've broken my spirit and spoiled my looks, and wot for" (131). (The accuracy yet inconsistency with which Mansfield recorded the backcountry dialect is evident.)

By the time the spring issue of *Rhythm* appeared, not only did this story and two Mansfield poems masquerading as translations of "Boris Petrovsky" occupy the lion's share of the magazine, but Katherine and Murry had met and their relationship was moving swiftly toward erratic permanence. On 11 April 1912, for seven shillings and six pence a week, Murry took lodgings in the "music room" of Mansfield's flat, a purely business arrangement to help Murry move away from home. Though Murry's account makes it seem that they lodged for a long time under the same roof like friendly, intellectual brothers, within a month they slept together and went happily to Paris to obtain J. D. Fergusson's blessing upon their union (*B2L,* 216).

Thus with the June issue (already a financial failure, *Rhythm* now changed publishers and irrationally became a monthly) the lion became one of a pair of Tigers, as Mansfield and Murry announced "The Meaning of Rhythm." For the first time there was a masthead listing Murry as editor "Assisted by: Katherine Mansfield and Michael T. H. Sadleir." The next month Sadleir's name was gone. Not till February 1913 was equality established with "Edited by John Middleton Murry and Katherine Mansfield." Despite denunciations from the *New Age,* which in June printed its last Mansfield piece for three years, *Rhythm* continued through March 1913. In May it became for three monthly issues the *Blue Review;* then it vanished from the literary scene. Mansfield also vanished from publication until she and Murry became involved during fall 1915 with the D. H. Lawrence–inspired *Signature,* a thin magazine which saw three issues in one month and then was done, having printed only the works of its three founders.

During these three and a half years Mansfield spent her energies on poetry, stories, critical articles, and reviews, as well as on the business affairs of the three little magazines edited by Murry. To help finance them, she sacrificed her annual allowance from her father. She supported herself by entertaining with comic songs or monologues at Mayfair tea parties and by acting as an extra in silent movies (Alpers, 71–72; *Letters,* 1:293). She published 14 stories in these periodicals and one in Frank Harris's *House and Home.* Inevitably she heard during this time a tremendous amount of talk about art. Restlessly she participated in it. But her own writing for these magazines exhibited little advance beyond her earlier work.

The noncritical writing begins in August and September with two false starts which have never been collected. Apparently attempts in the Russian manner, these stories are presumably supposed to be brutal—as the magazine required. "Tales of a Courtyard" consists of three sketches connected only by the cold setting. The first sketch (*Rhythm,* August 1912, 99–100) begins with a first-person-plural viewpoint, as dwellers in the courtyard rejoice in the coming of spring, but when they jeer at the outsider inmate, a Russian girl, the author has abandoned the original point of view. The fluctuation of emotion from pleasure through speculation to gloom and final derision is handled with economy. It is a description of the "democratic mob" scorned by the aristocratic artists of "Seriousness in Art."

Sketch 2, (*Rhythm,* August 1912, 100–102), "The Following After," has a dreamlike, feverish quality as a girl seeks Mark, who has angrily left her to "end the whole bloody business." Eventually she follows what may be his revenant to a room where he lies stiffly. Her mental state has been suggested somewhat in the manner of "The Child-Who-Was-Tired"; it is similarly hallucinatory from weariness, but is conveyed through intensely perceived color images (yellow street lights on white snow) which suggest that Mansfield's association with the Fauvist painters encouraged by *Rhythm* is intensifying her visual imagery. The sketch concludes with a typically ambiguous but "brutal" image: "She was so tired that for a moment she thought it was the sunrise staining the pillow so red."

In the third sketch, "By Moonlight," (*Rhythm,* August 1912, 102–105) Feodor sits on a snowy bench beside an old man who delights in a precious, beautiful book, which he will not sell despite his poverty. When he sleeps, Feodor steals it, suffers from conscience through the night, determines to return the book, but does not. In the morning the old man is found dead on the cold bench. The influence on plot and psychology is apparently that of Dostoyevsky, in a very much diluted fashion.

"Spring in a Dream," the effort of the following month, is Russian only in the names of the characters. More pity than brutality is displayed for the young cripple Michael, the recipient of inadequate sympathy from his relatives, who prefer the memory of his active, revolutionary youth. The center of interest lies in the increase of depth in the viewpoint character, from "he ought to realize that we have so short a holiday at home and no time to be eternally sympathetic" to her final perception of Michael weeping at his loss of strength: "And now the sun, shining through the front windows, painted on the bare floor the shadow of Michael with his lap full of fruit." This shadow, juxtaposing the broken man with the fulfillment of harvested fruit, gains in blunt strength, in contrast to the fragile opening image of the story, a shadow of chrysanthemums "too delicate and fine for the heavy room. . . . It quivered as though longing to go back and hide among the petals of the plants," causing the viewpoint character to speculate on "the terror of captive shadow." Again the work is strongly visual, but it manages through implication to convey compassionate irony. Perhaps the author is now looking at *Rhythm* reproductions of the refined, early drawings of Picasso rather than the stark, Fauvist decorations Anne Estelle Rice made for the magazine.

In the same issue appeared "How Pearl Button Was Kidnapped," an earlier work according to Murry's pre–*New Age* date of 1910. This wish-fulfillment account of a child stolen by Maoris, New Zealand's native inhabitants, rejects the ordinary conventional life from which *Rhythm,* despite its slogan of realism, recoils. Pearl innocently asks the Maoris, "Don't you all live in a row?. . . . Aren't there any nasty things?" But just as she has become ecstatically happy, the police come running toward her across the seashore, to return her to the House of Boxes. The entire story is seen from the viewpoint of a very young child. To create the impression of utter simplicity, Mansfield experiments in parataxis very successfully. It recurs in "Something Childish but Very Natural"; however, in her later portraits of children she never used the technique again, perhaps because the children were never again so innocent.

Elena, the child of "New Dresses," is a determined, rebellious, persecuted child. "Hellish!" she shouts, describing her environment to the sympathetic Doctor Erb (32).[3] Though the plot concerns the conflict of Elena with her parents, focused on her childish attempt to conceal the tearing of her new dress, the author's interest is diffused. A series of four episodes covering three days comments largely on the characters and relationships of the adults. Andreas Binzer, the father, is still parsimonious, inconsiderate, self-centered, and self-pitying. He is so "overcome" by Elena's stolid indifference to his appeals that he puts his outdoor boots on the starched bolster of his bed. His wife, very antagonistic to Elena, weeps at the story of her misbehavior. Her attitude fluctuates between resentment at her husband's attempts at economy (which she actually ignores) and appreciation of his fine looks and generosity. The grandmother seems to dote a little. Anna Binzer thinks so early in the story; the doctor, when she fails to appreciate that by repairing the dress he has saved Elena a whipping, agrees. The approach in which people are revealed from a variety of shifting viewpoints and by the implications of their own actions and responses foreshadows, as do the scene and analysis of family politics, "Prelude."

The last paragraph of the *Rhythm* version of "New Dresses" has been wisely excluded from the Murry edition. It followed Mansfield's early usual technique of unification, through the repetition of opening images about the dresses, deepened by other remarks that recall the themes of Elena's rebellion and her mother's extravagant indifference. The artifice is unnecessary to finish a story which, having opened in the middle of an environment where all is assumed to be familiar to the reader, should properly close on the musing evaluative comment of the doctor, returning the emphasis to the lack of adult understanding of a child's world.

As in the spring, Mansfield is again filling an issue, for she supplies in this one of October another story and a sketch. "The Little Girl" plays an intertextual counterpoint to a story by Murry, "The Little Boy," printed in August. Murry's story draws on childhood memory, brutalized, presumably to conform to *Rhythm* policy. It details the agony of a six-year-old in the care of a hag who beats him often with a leather strap. He fears alleys and corners, has nightmares over the decorations of a Christmas paper. Terrified, he apparently breaks his leg on the way to the old woman's room, where he wants to climb into her bed for comfort. She strikes him, and he crawls painfully down to the cellar and is left anticipating death with the rats.[4]

In "The Little Girl" Kass, renamed Kezia in Murry's later edition of Mansfield's stories, is in fear, not of alleys and corners but of her overwhelming, impatient, brusque, giantlike father. Innocently she tears up an important speech to make him a birthday present and is whipped on her hands with a ruler. Despite her grandmother's comforting (again the mother only leads the culprit to the father), her fear is confirmed, and she first questions "What did Jesus make fathers for?" (141) Then, from watching the playful father next door, she learns there are different sorts.

Left alone in the house with her father, she screams out in a nightmare, but the man takes her tenderly into bed with him, where she concludes that although he is too tired from hard work to be a playful father he has a big heart.

In contrast to Murry's pointless exaggeration, Mansfield's story develops a change in feeling in its viewpoint character. Except for two small lapses in Kass's interior monologue (in reference to her stuttering, she "had quite given it up," and she watches light through venetian blinds "trace a sad little pattern" [139, 140]), the diction consistently maintains the child's viewpoint and the structure is formally compact. The parallels in content suggest that the story was written as a mild, realistic corrective to Murry's excess.

"Sunday Lunch," not collected as a story, is merely a *New Age*–like attack on the malice of self-satisfied, materially successful dilettantes who consider themselves artists but are "not real enough to die" (*Scrapbook,* 14). This sardonic tone is typical of Mansfield's reviews, as when she ticks off Galsworthy's *Moods, Songs, and Doggerels* with "Mr. Galsworthy is wise in that he avoids all mention of the word 'poetry' in connexion with his verses."[5] This attitude contrasts strongly with Murry's typical adulation, for instance, in his extravagant praise of James Stephens and Frank Harris.[6]

"Ole Underwood" in January was the second of Mansfield's treatments of local color in the New Zealand backcountry, and her last story for *Rhythm.* Like "The Woman at the Store" with which she began in the magazine, it is violent in content and intensely visual in the bright hues of the postimpressionists and Fauvists.[7] A strong wind, an intensified heartbeat, and a red-and-white handkerchief are violently interrelated images, which seem to motivate Ole Underwood's reactions. Continually he sees red and his heart beats "madly." A crazy outcast, he experiences a moment of tenderness for a stray cat, recalling his faithless but beloved wife; then, in revulsion, he tosses the cat into the sewer and apparently goes on board a ship. But the ending is hallucinatory. The man on the bunk with his head on a red pillow (recalling the closing image of the second of the "Tales of a Courtyard") may be the sailor (lover of his wife) whom he killed long ago, a vision of his past self, or an innocent stranger whom Ole Underwood is about to kill. This deliberate ambiguity fittingly completes the portrait within his deranged viewpoint. In the bold strokes of color and harsh style appropriate to the madman, Mansfield provides a sharp corrective to the domestic stories of little girls.

The *New Age* (28 March 1912) had hailed "The Woman at the Store" as "defiant of the rules of art, for it ploughs the realistic sand, with no single relief of wisdom or wit." Of "Ole Underwood" it said: "Miss Mansfield makes an inartistic stink with a dirty old imbecile who murders cats" (6 February 1913). But when the *Blue Review* replaced *Rhythm*, though disapproval of the publication continued—"Can the leopard change its spots?"—the *New Age* was delighted with "Pension Séguin": "the best work she has done since she left us for an editorial feather in her cap. . . . She has made amends. . . . Here is work which we are very pleased indeed to welcome" (15 May 1913). The reason for such approval is obvious: in this story—and in two to follow, "Violet" and "Bains Turcs"—Mansfield has returned to her German pension manner and is writing the type of story that the *New Age* editorial policy encouraged. The editors recognized their own when they saw it. The title under which the stories originally appeared, "Epilogues" 1, 2, and 3 may have been intended to recall the earlier success.

Now the pressure of journalistic work appears for the first time in Mansfield's letters: "Such a relief that Ive written my reviews again and started my epilogue." A month earlier she wrote, "I've nursed the epilogue to no purpose. Every time I pick it up and hear 'youll keep it to six,' I *cant* cut it. To my knowledge there arent any superfluous words: I mean every line of it. . . . I'd rather it wasn't there at all than sitting in the Blue Review with a broken nose and one ear as though it had jumped into an editorial dogfight." And the next letter: "P.S. I dont know whether you will roar at me, darling for doing the books in this way. But they lent themselves to it & I thought if you read the review you would see that its almost silly to notice them singly & that they gain like this. If wrong—return the thing & I'll do you 2 little ones" (*Letters*, 1:124–25, 127). She won. "Violet" (epilogue 2) remained six and a half pages, and two books appeared in one review.

Of the three *New-Age*–style stories, only the third, "Bains Turcs," in a sudden revelation of concealed character, has a degree of depth. All are clever wit but of insignificant value. Essentially they criticize humanity in something akin to the manner Mansfield had decried in "Sunday Lunch." The one development is that, at last, the viewpoint character, so supercilious in *In a German Pension,* has begun to laugh at herself. As "Pension Séguin" (epilogue 1) begins, she introduces her peculiar fright on entering the boardinghouse as "ridiculous," which it certainly is. Her immediate antagonism to the place and to the people is as unmotivated as in the earlier stories, and the fluctuation of attitude is less motivated than in "Frau Brechenmacher Attends a Wedding." After a sardonic rumination on the white mats which dominate the salon, she suddenly sees them as "tokens of virtue and sobriety," and philosophically defending her belief in appearances, she takes the room for two months. Courage has metaphorically fled "like a disobedient dog (148–50)." Contrary to expectation the place is a bedlam. M. Seguin looks like a rat; the most wicked of the badly behaved children is significantly named Hélène like the "bad" child in "New Dresses"; and the conversation is banal. The climax dispels her belief in appearances; the mats were made by the lady on the first floor. Mansfield has returned to the Chekhovian joke pattern.

"Violet" continues at the pension, opening with the awakening of the self-conscious pensioner who admires her own fanciful imagery in the manner of the later Raoul Duquette. She imagines herself defending the truth of proverbs, be they ever so unctuous and irritating, against an imagined Katherine Tynan's whimsical arguments. Looking out the window, the pensioner is a sentimental daydreamer, awakened to reality by a servant beating rugs. She knows her sober breakfast reflections are both "pious and smug." Then, as in "A Truthful Adventure," comes the chance meeting with an old friend, Violet, who has a romantic secret to reveal. Delayed by the witty oppositions of the pensioner, Violet finally reveals that her experience of the "pinnacles . . . and depths" consists of her recent seven dances, long talk, and final kiss from a man who immediately confessed that he was engaged. "Is that all?" (157–59) cries the letdown confident, and knows that the sound of the fountain "half sly, half laughing" (this is a repeated image, the usual unifying device) is laughing at her (153–59). Except for consistent self-mockery, there is no necessary relationship between the beginning and the end. Perhaps the story could not have been cut by one-half page, but it could have been split in two.

"Bains Turcs" (epilogue 3) has the natural unity of consisting entirely of observations which could have been and probably were made at a Turkish bath. They begin with the usual repugnance for ugly human beings and continue to a choice of daydreams brought on by the odors of the Warm Room. Mockery of the other inmates is voiced in the amused conversation of two stout blonds, who are especially entertained by the inability of a German, named, for the nonce, Mackintosh Cap, to get service from the French attendant. Although the German-and-French-speaking viewpoint character could have helped her but did not, Mackintosh Cap begins a conversation in the Hot Room. She wants a sympathetic hearer; though the pensioner is withdrawn, Mackintosh Cap thinks she has an audience simply because the language barrier is broken. She denounces the attendant and is resolved not to tip. She asserts that the blonds are not respectable. Their insulting laughter has ruined her sweat. She also manages to mention modesty, domestic duties, and her five children, one born dead, all produced in six years of marriage. Most of what Mansfield dislikes about the Germans has been epitomized in this woman. In the anteroom as all depart, the blonds are indeed attractive in "charming feathered hats and furs," as opposed to the German woman's "terrible bird nest . . . *Reise-hut.*" But there is effected a brilliantly swift turn of impression. Mackintosh Cap comments, "how do you suppose they can afford clothes like that?" Then she "stared after them, her sallow face all mouth and eyes, like the face of a hungry child before a forbidden table" (159–64). The imaginings of the prudish, desirous Mackintosh Cap may suggest her latent lesbianism.[8] With this closing Mansfield has finally reached her top pitch in achieving the objectives of *Rhythm:* a brutal analysis of the woman's motive for her calumniations, inextricably blended with the author's sudden flash of insight and consequent pity.

It has become customary to treat the three stories of New Zealand "outback" together, despite chronology, merely because they treat similar subjects and are essentially untypical of Mansfield's work. In terms of technique, however, "Millie" is more akin to "Bains Turcs," with the same sudden turn of awareness and penetration into human complexity at the end. Millie seems to be a hard, ignorant, crude woman. Willfully childless, she is unexpectedly moved when she finds an injured young man behind the woodpile. Realizing that he is the murderer her husband and other men are away looking for, she determines to help him because "Men is all beasts" but " 'E's nothink but a sick kid" (145–46).

That night, after the men have returned and are in bed, she lies rigid, hoping the young man will now escape: "I don' care anythink about justice an' all the rot they've bin spoutin' to-night." The question bears ironically on her own lack of self-knowledge, for she is to take a second unexpected turn. When the dog barks and pursuit begins again, first she is horrified. But then "a strange mad joy smothered everything else. She rushed into the road—she laughed and shrieked and danced in the dust. 'Arter 'im, Sid! . . . Shoot 'im down.'" (147). This is the only backwoods story in which complexity of character is examined.

In this sudden onset of bloodlust there is a raw kinship with Viola of "The Swing of the Pendulum." One moment she is playing the childish game of charades with a strange man; in the next, fighting him off, she bites him and rejoices at his pain. Stimulated by the fray, she then becomes again her sentimental self. The feeling is related too to that of the *Scrapbook* Kezia of 1916, who smiles, though also still frightened, remembering that on the previous evening, standing up to her father for the first time, she called him "Bottlenose" (*Scrapbook*, 50). The intensity of Matilda in the *Signature* "Autumn II" was not modified five years later when the story was rewritten slightly as "The Wind Blows" for the *Athenaeum*. Matilda, defying her mother and full of fury, still rushes out into the wind shouting "Go to hell" (216). Though her expressions became tamer, Mansfield did not lose interest in latent human violence. Many of her stories study cruelty and its effects until, in the end, "The Fly" offers an overwhelming analysis of the impulse.

When the *Blue Review* failed in July, Mansfield suffered a creative lull. She would not publish again until the October and November 1915 issues of the *Signature*. In December she and Murry moved to Paris, where she was able to stay until the end of February. While there she wrote "Something Childish But Very Natural," not published until 1924. This story, with "An Indiscreet Journey" and a first-draft beginning of "The Aloe," fills the two-year interlude before D. H. Lawrence interested Mansfield and Murry in the brief-lived *Signature*.

For the moment not writing for any magazine, limited by neither the demands of space nor editorial policy, Mansfield produced a story more than twice as long as her usual one, and far more carefully wrought. She replaced the sudden flash of insight exposed in an unexpected final image with the detailed development of sensitively perceived feeling. Her purpose is that the reader should come to know and understand through its process the innocent longing, sweetness, and pain of an adolescent love affair. It was hardly calculated to appeal to her literary friends and was not published until after her death.

Her evaluative challenge lies in the title—"Something Childish But Very Natural." It was childish of Edna to withdraw so repeatedly from Henry's chaste advances, but because she was 16 it was also natural. It was childish too of 17-year-old Henry to arrange, in his longing, to play house with Edna, but again, very natural. Their whole delicate, fanciful love affair was childish, an affair truly of children, but it was as natural as any of the more violent outpourings of the naturalistic school, perhaps more natural, and certainly built to convey a tenderer sympathy.

The tale seems deceptively simple at first. It moves straightforwardly through the initial meeting of the pair, a few typical encounters, and the two fresh childlike love letters, to the day when Edna fails to come to the cottage Henry has rented. But the design pronounces this more than a disaster of childhood; it is a failure of faith. Though she handles the story entirely from Henry's point of view, Mansfield takes particular care that Edna, who fails, shall be understood. At that second meeting on the train Edna sits stiffly; her hands tremble; she won't let Henry touch her hair and moves "a little away from him" in a dark railroad, tunnel. In the concert hall she won't let Henry help her with her coat and insists on holding the program to read to herself. Henry wonders,

> Why did he want to touch her so much and why did she mind?. . . . All the time that he was away from her he was hungry, he craved the near-ness of her. (173)

Here is natural passion registered on an innocent mind.

Edna sees him brooding and promises to "explain something" after the concert, but she loses her nerve for a moment and tries to leave him, foreshadowing her later dereliction. Then she recovers the courage to try to explain. She is aware that her evasions are hurting Henry, but natu-rally, she cannot help it: "Somehow I feel if once we did that—you know—held each other's hands and kissed it would be all changed. . . . We wouldn't be children any more . . . silly, isn't it?" While she speaks, "behind her as in a dream he saw the sky and half a white moon and the trees of the square with their unbroken buds"—images which symboli-cally confirm her remarks. At this point Henry promises to "bury the bogy in this square" (174–75), and they begin a childish but natural attempt to live unnaturally, as if they were, indeed, in a dream.

"London became their playground." Sentence rhythm and repetitions reinforce the childlike pretense of their activities: "They found their own shops . . . and their own tea-shop with their own table—their own streets—and one night . . . they found their own village." Everything is fancifully small. The words *little, small, tiny* repeat themselves with every new discovery. One house Henry would like to live in, and Edna agrees "with a dreamy smile." They weave a fantasy of their childlike married life in this house, even including the little cat that comes through the fence. But suddenly Henry wants to leave because "it's going to turn into a dream" (175–77). He fears the dream in a very real way, for on another day he says to Edna, who continues to wear her "strange,

dreamy smile," "Long after you have stopped laughing . . . I can hear
your laugh running up and down my veins—and yet—are we a dream?
And suddenly he saw himself and Edna as two very small children. . . .
He wanted to kiss Edna . . . until he'd no breath left and so stiffle the
dream" (178–79). After tea, where Henry tells the proprietor that Edna
is his sister, they investigate a "tiny" cottage which is for rent. Edna leans
against Henry, lets him embrace her though her voice is shaky, and finally tells him that she has "quite got over the feeling" (181).

In the next scene Henry has rented and prepared the cottage and is
waiting for Edna. "I don't believe this for a minute," he thinks, but Edna
earlier has said, "You have faith, haven't you?" So now he anticipates her
coming, their supper, even their going to bed, childishly, in separate
rooms, for it is still only a playhouse. Sitting on the doorstep, he recalls
her question: " 'Haven't you faith, Henry?' 'I hadn't then. Now I have,'
he said, 'I feel just like God' " (181–82). There is pathetic irony in this
declaration.

The climax of the story unfolds like the dream he feared, for Henry
falls asleep and sleepily thinks he sees a white moth coming down the
road. On their second meeting he had said to Edna, " 'I believe I've swal-
lowed a butterfly—and it's fanning its wings just here.' He put his hand
on his heart" (170). Now the white moth becomes a little girl with a
telegram. Henry remains in a dream as he speculates, "Perhaps it's only a
make-believe one, and it's got one of those snakes inside it that fly up at
you." Mansfield does not reveal the real snake that jumped out, but the
insects, which symbolically suggest the state of the soul, are trapped in
the implied image of the final paragraph: "The garden became full of
shadows—they span a web of darkness over the cottage and the trees
and Henry and the telegram. But Henry did not move" (182–83).

Henry, as his acquaintance with Edna began, had explained that they
had found each other by being natural. He added, "That's all life is—
something childish and very natural. Isn't it?" and Edna agreed (171).
But in the end, after Henry found faith, she rejected it and returned him
to the dream, which is not life and not natural. The final position of
Henry, dreaming in darkness lest he awake alone, exactly echoes the second and third stanzas of the Coleridge poem whence he acquired his philosophy and with which the story began:

> But in my sleep to you I fly,
> I'm always with you in my sleep,
>
> . . . .

> But then one wakes and where am I?
> All, all alone.
>
> . . . .
>
> For though my sleep be gone,
> Yet while 'tis dark one shuts one's lids,
> And so, dreams on.
>
>   (165; my ellipses)

The name of the poem is "Something Childish but Very Natural." While Henry waits for Edna, he remembers only the opening three optimistic lines: "Had I but two little wings, / And were a little feathery bird, / To you I'd fly, my dear—." The rest of the stanza, "But thoughts like these are idle things, / And I stay here," is the denial—the warning which from the beginning he has ignored.

The structure of this apparently simple story turns out to be intricate; it is built to move the reader through an interplay of images and rhythms, and a design of ironic echoes. Mansfield has taken great pains to convey, without sentimentality, an experience almost too delicate to communicate. Employing Henry's viewpoint, she maintains the necessary objectivity and control.

Murry, publishing the story after Mansfield's death, said that it was "refused by every editor to whom she submitted it" (*SS*, vi), but I have found no other evidence that she sought publication. I suspect that it was intended as a private message to Murry,[9] immediately responding to her situation in February 1914 in Paris, where she wrote the story.

In a fictional gender reversal, Mansfield identifies with the naive but passionately desirous, frustrated Henry and portrays in Edna the sexual frigidity of Murry, who began, with a telegram, the betrayal of their effort to set up permanent housekeeping in Paris. On 10 February, immediately on receiving the telegram, Mansfield replied, "I am afraid I am rather childish about people coming and going—and just, now, at this moment when the little boy has handed me your telegram—the disappointment is hard to bear" (*Letters*, 1:13).

In the story Henry's waiting in the rented cottage, where he imagines them sleeping in separate bedrooms after bidding each other a formal goodnight (182), parallels Murry's account of himself as boarder in Mansfield's Clovelly Mansions flat. He records that they always shook hands and said "goodnight" before they went to bed.

During an evening conversation he "expounded [his] new conviction that falling in love was a mistake." Mansfield responded with noncommittal questions, which to a less obtuse young man would have expressed doubt. Of an earlier love affair with the French Margueritte (whom he abandoned), Murry said, "That [making love] spoiled everything, somehow." Another evening, when Mansfield offered to become his mistress, he repeated the sentiment: "I feel it would spoil—everything" (*B2W,* 202, 205–6).

The fictitious Edna/Murry, rejecting Henry/Mansfield's advances, says, ". . . [I]f once we did that . . . we wouldn't be children anymore" (174–75). In *Still Life,* the novel Murry began in Paris and finished the next year in London, his concept of married life is still the same. When his surrogate Morry Temple and Mrs. Craddock marry, at first "they sleep in separate rooms."[10]

The spring before the Paris venture, when Mansfield was living in Cholesbury and Murry commuting from London on weekends, around 12 May 1913 he wrote, "O Tig, you were so sweet, and so like a child that I feel like crying when I write."[11] Often Mansfield accommodated Murry, assuming the childlike role he preferred to cast her in, but at this moment she wrote, "I cannot quite believe that you are coming back here. I feel—quite alone and as if I were writing to someone in the air—so strange." The letter began, ". . . . the postman knocked into my dream with your letter and the backdoor key" (*Letters,* 1:21–22; Mansfield's ellipsis.)

In Paris it is the same, but her doubt has become more defined. The day after the disappointing telegram she wrote again: "Did you take a return ticket. Would you rather stay on now and manage things by letter? Would you rather save the money?" (*Letters,* 1:137).

The story asserts that a couple who play or fantasize about setting up housekeeping, while one of them rejects a vital sexual relationship, are unreal and childish. Generously, using the Coleridge poem, the disasterous part of which Henry could not remember, Mansfield also calls it "natural." (She will use the poem with bitter intent in the later "Poison.") It is unlikely that Murry ever understood the message, as he later failed to understand "*Je ne Parle pas Français,*" "The Man without a Temperament," and who knows how many other stories.

Mansfield continued to confirm her doubts about Murry in the unproductive year which followed the Paris fiasco. Reading his private journal, she learned he had told Gordon Campbell that he did not know whether she was "more to him than a gratification" (Alpers, 171). On 18 December 1914 she wrote in her *Journal* (62–63), "That decides me–that frees me. I'll play this game no longer. . . . He has made me feel like a girl. I've loved, loved just like any girl,–but I'm not a girl, and these feelings are not mine. . . . He doesn't know me."

Already she had admired "the warm sensational life" emanating from letters Francis Carco was writing from the warring front lines in France (*Journal,* 62). At Carco's invitation, in February 1915 she undertook a risky, illegal journey to meet Carco at Gray, near the French western front. By 20 February she was recording the adventure in what is now known as notebook 4 in the Alexander Turnbull Library Mansfield collection.[12]

Though she was experimenting with the possibility of leaving the passionless Murry, he remained her best audience. She returned in ten days, having spent four with Carco and the rest traveling or in Paris. From the notebook she carried, both "letters" became a preliminary draft of the middle of "An Indiscreet Journey." Comparison of these jottings with the story provides a first glimpse of Mansfield's working methods.

To the reworked material Mansfield has added a beginning and an end, unified by religious imagery which the journal notes lack. Opening in Paris with gloomy warnings by a concierge who looks like St. Anne, mother of the Blessed Virgin Mary, the writer gradually intensifies the sense of risk, contrasting it with the first-person narrator's jaunty daring or distancing of fear through bravado and self-mockery. This tension coheres with conflicting observations from the train, views of the destructive ugliness of war in the context of beautiful color and scenery. Soldiers' blue-and-red uniforms are "ridiculous like bright irreverent transfers." Each guard she sees "like a little comic picture waiting for the joke to be written underneath." But with this image begins the counterpoint theme, for the passage continues: "Is there really such a thing as war? Are all these laughing voices really going to the war? These dark woods lighted so mysteriously by the white stems of the birch and the ash—these watery fields with the big birds flying over—these rivers green and blue in the light—have battles been fought in places like these?" (185).

And she observes the "beautiful" cemeteries, gay and full of flowers she thinks at first, but no: they are ribbons tied onto soldiers' graves. It is, in fact, disbelief that her gaiety reflects. She cannot take in the reality of war, which can only appear absurd in the context of "darling" soldiers and their "ridiculous" uniforms. The officials she must delude are also ridiculous. The peak of her necessary but absurd terror is reflected in her unnerved readiness to kneel to these pompous, powerful men, whom she calls God 1 and God 2.

The repeated religious imagery conveys her vision of the French at war. Opening in an observation of her concierge as St. Anne, the traveler sees herself derisively through the eyes of the calamity-predicting Frenchwoman. At a buffet where she must change trains, the humble presence of an old man with a bucket of fish, looking "as though he had escaped from some holy picture, and was entreating the soldiers' pardon for being there at all". The fisherman of the notebook now suggests St. Peter. His image (186), challenges the world of war and leaves the viewpoint character with a guilty feeling that she should have bought the fish, if only to throw them away. And at the end of the story, as the customers of a café silently listen to the military police pass after closing time, "the faces lifted, listening. 'How beautiful they are!' I thought. "They are like a family party having supper in the New Testament (197).' " It is the beauty of these "Warriors" which in every case belies the reality of war and renders its concerns a monstrous absurdity.

The insistence of this imagery is intensified by several changes from notebook tone. From the balance of terror and nervous wit in the first section, the story turns to the more realistic observation of soldiers near the front. Wounded men are seen petting a miserable dog. In a café amid the casual complaints of soldiers and the distractions of drink and card-playing, a man sits uncontrollably weeping, his eyes just unbandaged from an injury. The man groans from time to time, but the other men, quarreling and laughing over their game, pay no attention to what is commonplace in their experience. Only the proprietress is finally compelled to comment that it's rather unpleasant to which they casually agree (194).

The final section, none of which is in the notebook, focuses on the intensity with which one man, "the blue-eyed soldier," insists upon finding a very special drink for the English girl. The half-drunk conversation and the trivial goal of the insistent quest, which, like the girl's journey, involves an indiscreet challenging of army regulations, end the story. The group is drinking in a dirty scullery to avoid being caught by the police. But the voice of the blue-eyed soldier is happy in the dark, and he pronounces the *mirabelle,* a plum cordial, "excellent—*ex-cellent.*" This closing on a small satisfaction is tonally controlled by the recurrent religious symbolism; it recalls for the reader that—though now in the dark and pursuing small, temporary satisfactions—these people have a beauty that is somehow reminiscent of holiness.

Mansfield's use of religious imagery to envision men at war precedes by at least two years "the sacrificial theme in which each soldier becomes a type of the crucified Christ," found by Paul Fussell "at the heart of countless Great War poems." He attributes the prevalence of the image to the presence of crossroad shrines, "the numerous real physical calvaries visible at French and Belgian crossroads."[13] Mansfield, on her long train ride south beyond Paris to Châteaudan, then east to Gray, must have seen them.

At the time of this writing Mansfield was strongly opposed to excess spirituality; however, in this story, without any overt statement, maintaining her objectivity through the consciousness of a rather frivolous yet sensitive observer, she manages to surround her soldiers with compassionate vision and thus to underline the ugly "joke" too many of them were waiting for. The action of the story too supports this motif. It is almost entirely taken up with alternately waiting and trying to get somewhere. There is waiting for trains, for food, for a companion, for the approval of officials, and for the police to pass. And through this waiting one sees continually soldiers and occasional civilians, all confronting the war by waiting and by passing time as if they were doing something else.

For, sitting in a café, the narrator can feel that years have passed and "Perhaps the war is long since over—there is no village outside at all—the streets are quiet under the grass," and it seems like the "very last day of all", by implication Judgment Day (192). Only the entrance of the proprietress and the soldiers brings her back to reality, a waiting for another reality which she cannot experience, cannot, indeed, realize, but must somehow defy in her view of the simplicity and beauty of these people, so absurdly, so impossibly out of place, as she is, in a wartime setting.

Her brother Leslie Beauchamp, in England for his military service, had provided the money for the real indiscreet journey into France (*B2W*, 324). Conversations with him through the spring and summer of 1915 stirred the recollections embodied in "Autumns" 1 and 2 (later entitled "The Apple Tree" and "The Wind Blows"), and published in the October issues of *Signature*.

This publication, a short-lived fiasco, was intended by Lawrence to be the mouthpiece for a group he hoped to lead toward religious and social reform. Disaffection was immediately evident in the name of the publication, which Murry chose in order to indicate that the contributors took "no responsibility for one another's creeds." Each man composed his philosophy and each "broke off in the middle." Of his own, Murry later wrote, "I confess that I barely understand it" (*B2W,* 348–50, 353, 357). Meanwhile Mansfield, utterly unsympathetic toward the clamoring verbosity of either man, published three stories, none of them the "little satirical sketches" Lawrence expected (Alpers, 181).

"The Little Governess," though printed last, was probably written first. In form it follows a young woman through a day of travel and sightseeing and is thus akin to "An Indiscreet Journey," but the young woman through whose mind the adventure is experienced is now naive, romantic, innocently ignorant. Warned by the lady at the employment bureau which sent her abroad, she is wisely fearful at the beginning of her trip. But Mansfield creates from the outset in the reader an ambivalent attitude toward that advice which would have kept the young girl safe. The lady's remarks, as recalled by the little governess, seem exaggerated: "[I]f you get into a compartment for 'Ladies Only' in the train you will be far safer than sleeping in a foreign hotel. Don't go out of the carriage. . . . It's better to mistrust people at first rather than trust them, and it's safer to suspect people of evil intentions rather than good ones" (201). Out of these remarks spring the ironies of the story. The reader, amused by the excessive precautions, is also entertained by the girl's fluctuating feelings of security and fear. In her encounter with the porter she is dutifully, ridiculously mistrustful. Following her instructions, she requests a carriage for women only, and in her obedience to these two admonitions begins her downfall. Angered by an innocently inadequate tip, the porter places a lascivious old man in her compartment. Because he contrasts with the boisterous, flirtatious young men in the next carriage, she departs injudiciously from her instructions and allows the old man to strike up a conversation. Her arrival at her Munich hotel with this old man reasonably arouses the suspicions of a waiter. Though his insult might have warned her, she takes it for insolence; again, in ignorance of tipping conventions, she antagonizes this man who will complete her ruin. The extent of the waiter's alienation is stressed in a sudden change of view-point at the end of the story, when he triumphs, with a heartbeat mad enough to recall Ole Underwood.

A deft structure involves the reader in condoning the ignorant girl's failure to take good advice. Moreover, since the menacing waiter and porter are described from her point of view, the reader might even be compelled to sympathize with her on their account. And again, as she

gradually comes to think of the old man as "grandfather," the reader
may unsuspectingly agree, though his German title and his recollections
of travel to Turkey and attar of roses should remind the Mansfield adept
of the mockery of Herr Rat in "Frau Fischer." It is hard, however, to
maintain sympathy with the girl's excessive joy. Her limitations are
revealed in her language: what she likes is "nice," "wonderful." Finally,
as she sits with her back to the clock, already too late to meet her
prospective employer, Mansfield intensifies the foolishness of the immature girl, who has misinterpreted, through stereotypical vision, her experience of the day. The deliberately cloyed language, expressive of her
consciousness, persuades me that Mansfield does not sympathize with
this victim. Though glancing at the evil aggressions of porters and waiters (a bête noire of the traveling Mansfield), intensified by the sexually
exploitative old man, the ironic theme remains the advantage of following the excessively good, mocked advice.[14] Mansfield has rendered the
woman from the Government Bureau correct and the reader, if deluded
on that point, perhaps surprised by this outcome.

The technique of "The Apple Tree" is not characteristic. It is a
straightforward recollection of an incident in the New Zealand childhood, in which there is apparently no effort to fictionize. The first-person
narrator is omniscient; instead of carrying on the usual interior monologue or being concerned with defining her own attitudes, she has pene-
trated into direct analysis of her father and identifies the little brother
Bogey with herself. The materialistic, sensitive father, who "still won-
dered whether in the deepest sense he got his money's worth," is told by
an English visitor that the fruit of the tree—"the accidental thing—the
thing that no one had been aware of when the hard bargain was driven,
[which] . . . hadn't in a way been paid for"—is highly valued. The children, threatened with whipping if they touch the fruit, are able to share
a little ironic triumph at harvest time. "Perfect," they say, when stingily
granted a taste: thus they leave their father to experience for himself "a
floury stuff, a hard, faintly bitter skin—a horrible taste of something
dry." The "strange meaning smile" they exchange contradicts the final
paragraph, which suggests that the children lied to protect their father's
feelings (*Journal,* 86–89).

"The Wind Blows," a sketch, is to some extent written in the same
manner. For publication in *Bliss,* the first-person narrator was changed to
third person, effecting an entrance into Matilda's consciousness. The
wind and the depression and excitement it arouses in the adolescent
account for images and unity. There are several shifts in tone: a fright-

ened awakening at the noise of the wind, a mood in which all its effects are destructive and the realities of life (a phone call from the butcher) ugly, and then the contrasting quiet of a piano studio where the feeling that the music teacher is sympathetic causes tears. It may be that his sympathy is a ploy, inviting her to sexual intimacy. A minor ironic note is introduced when the music teacher greets the next student with the same phrase he used to welcome Matilda.

Despite that peaceful lull, Matilda, alone again in her bedroom with the wind still blowing, is fearful and recalcitrant in her isolation. Relief and understanding reappear when her brother proposes a walk to the esplanade. The girl bids farewell to her reflection in a mirror; at the dock, seeing a ship departing, she imagines they are both on board. Her perspective shifts to a position on the ship with Bogey many years later as she calls on him to remember and bids the little island good-bye. The final awareness is of the wind.[15] The story appeared on 18 October 1915, 11 days after Leslie Beauchamp was killed in France. Probably the fantasy ending is related to the intense grief Katherine Mansfield felt at this time.

The stories of the little-magazine period are generally more strongly plotted than those of *In a German Pension:* only four of the twelve later stories are episodes, as against nine of the twelve in the earlier work. This contrast between the two groups is even more conspicuous in that it differs strongly from Mansfield's later practice. There are only four plots in the fourteen stories of *Bliss*; only one, in the fifteen of *The Garden Party*.

The stories of this little-magazine period rarely take comic form, and less than half are caustic. The narrators are almost evenly divided between first- and third-person participants in the action, with shifting viewpoints in two stories. They are more sympathetic than the prejudiced girl of *In a German Pension*, and there is a beginning of change in attitude during their stories. Mansfield is nearing the discovery of the value of a fallible narrator, a technique used so far to characterize Andreas Binzer and the little governess. This change in the narrator's capacities is a necessary technical reflection of increasing depth of awareness in the writer. In the surprising turns of "Bains Turcs" and "Millie," still akin in pattern to the Chekhovian joke style of the *Pension*, comes revelation of the complexity of human motives. But the advances of the magazine pieces are slight. The greatest value of the experience is probably that it kept the writer at work in the exploration of her craft.

Chapter Four

"The Turning Point"

J. M. Murry has described as effecting the turning point in Katherine Mansfield's career the experience of renewed relationship with her brother Leslie and then the shock of his death: "The crucial moment was when, in 1915, her dearly loved younger brother arrived in England to serve as an officer. Her meeting with him formed, as it were, a point around which her changed attitude [a turn to childhood memories, "uncontaminated by the mechanical civilization which had produced the war"] could crystalize. . . . [she] resolved to dedicate herself to recreating life as she had lived and felt it in New Zealand."[1]

Conversations with Leslie were, of course, the immediate impulse which initiated "The Apple Tree," "The Wind Blows," and finally "Prelude." But treatments of New Zealand memories were not unusual for Mansfield. In her first *New Age* period "A Birthday" and "The Breidenbach Family in England" present her family, thinly disguised with German names. Four of her *Rhythm* stories have a New Zealand setting, as does "Millie" for the *Blue Review*. The subject matter of her work, early and late, rises almost entirely from her experience: the New Zealand girlhood, the bohemian world of literary London, the Continental world in which she so frequently convalesced, and occasionally her dreams. Of the fourteen stories in *Bliss,* two recall New Zealand; of the fifteen in *The Garden Party,* six do so. It never dominates as a source of material, despite the intention expressed in the journal entry of 22 January 1916, "to write about my own country till I simply exhaust my store" (*Journal,* 93–94).

This same entry has been taken as evidence of a sharp change in the form and manner of her stories. She wrote, at the moment, "[T]he form that I would choose has changed utterly. I feel no longer concerned with the same appearance of things. The people who lived or whom I wished to bring into my stories don't interest me any more. The plots of my stories leave me perfectly cold" (*Journal,* 93).

But this disavowal cannot be read as defining Mansfield's literary course. It expresses her enthusiasm as she is at work on an early draft of "Prelude." Two years later, in a letter of 14 February 1918, she felt similarly about "Je ne Parle pas Français": "Trouble is I feel I have found an *approach* to a story now which I must apply to everything. Is that nonsense? I read what I wrote before that . . . & I feel: no, this is all *once removed:* It wont do. And it wont. Ive got to reconstruct everything" (*Letters*, 2:71–72). And while she is not completely right in either case— no writer is likely to appraise herself accurately when in the process of composition—a more conspicuous technical innovation is marked by "Je ne Parle pas" than by "Prelude."

In both stories Mansfield was discovering a more dramatic and a more lyric form. Her subjective outlook carried her to a more intense mode of lyricism than that of her avowed master Chekhov. Where Chekhov narrates generalities, Mansfield dramatizes particulars. Where he describes typical family life in a typical provincial town, she portrays a specific family in a precisely detailed location. Chekhov deals with Russia and humanity; Mansfield writes of her own life and her immediate emotional response to it. The result in "Prelude" is a short story much removed from the Chekhovian form she so admired.

To increase dramatic as opposed to narrative quality, Mansfield had frequently experimented with detaching herself, the author, from the story. In the early stories this objectivity had been achieved largely by including a first-person narrator who participated in the action. Two variations had moved the stories toward more dramatic form. The first-person narrator is fallible in "Pension Séguin," and several stories are told largely from the viewpoint of a third-person participant. The most successful in this mode before "Something Childish" are the very early "Tiredness of Rosabel" (the omniscient narrator interprets at the end), "A Birthday" (there is a brief shift to the viewpoint of the servant girl, suggesting an omniscient narrator), "Ole Underwood," "The Little Girl," and "Millie."[2] "The Little Governess," written at about the same time as *The Aloe,* employs a third-person, fallible narrator—a device that is technically the greatest advance toward dramatic method. In most of these attempts, however, the diction fails to maintain the limitations which should be imposed by the character of the fictional narrator. Not yet free of writing for Murry, Mansfield cannot yet achieve the impersonality she aspires to.

But she is on the way. In order to reflect the action of "Prelude" through many minds, Mansfield returns to an omniscient perspective. The vantage point is used to adopt a number of viewpoints; there is no intrusion, no comment by the author. The larger excisions from the original version, *The Aloe,* eliminate excessive New Zealand detail and

account of tthe grandmother, not immediately relevant to the present-
ness in time of the story. The backgrounds of the Samuel Josephs family
or of Linda Burnell's girlhood serve no purpose in the work as finally
conceived. Though known to an omniscient author, they have no place
in the consciousnesses to which that author has limited herself. Thus the
final story seems to flow only through the minds of those present as the
immediate action elicits their perception. And all of these minds expose
themselves, like a cluster of infallible narrators, telling the story from
what Erich Auerbach has called a "multipersonal viewpoint."[3]

In this type of shift from mind to mind, with the author apparently
eliminated, Mansfield continues until time too is controlled by her men-
talities—as in the free fluctuations of "The Daughters of the Late
Colonel." She has discovered the maximum value of the single fallible
viewpoint, which controls her second major type of story, in "Je ne Parle
pas Français."

No matter what abstract studies in technique may reveal, discovery
for the artist lies ultimately in performance. The approach Mansfield
hailed with so much excitement after she wrote "Je ne Parle pas
Français" was merely an increase in the fallibility and the distancing of
the narrator. For the first time, she portrayed a narrator for whom she
felt no sympathy but distinct distaste. That Raoul Duquette tells of the
abandoning of the gentle, frightened, courageous Mouse increases the
horror of her position and the reader's contempt for him. The very form
of the story serves to surround Mouse with depravity.

Before this story could be written and while *The Aloe* was being
reworked into "Prelude," Mansfield wrote at least eight pieces for the
New Age. One appeared 4 November 1915; the others in May, June,
September, and October 1917. Of these, one was a translation from
Daudet, three were published in *Bliss,* and one, "The Common Round,"
was rewritten as "Pictures" for the same volume. The others, more or
less like little plays, are of interest as transitional experiments in dramatic form. "Late at Night" is pure monologue; "Stay-Laces" and "Two
Tuppenny Ones, Please," monologues with stage directions for silent but
excited responses of the speaker's companion; "The Black Cap," dia-
logues shifting through five scenes. "In Confidence" and "A Picnic" con-
fusedly combine short story and play techniques. In the need of the last
three to break through the limitations of dialogue and stage directions,
and in the relative freedom of monologue, Mansfield probably found her
way to the interior monologue of "Mr. Reginald Peacock's Day," in
which the omniscient author is almost entirely effaced. The self-con-

scious artificialities of Peacock's character also point the way to "Je ne Parle pas Français."

An examination of the way Mansfield, with a few scenic transitions, changed the bare dialogue of "The Common Round" into the short story "Pictures" reveals how she may have transformed oral performance into fictional progress through a single consciousness. Each addition to the dialogue removes the original abrupt jumps from place to place as Ada Moss tours agents and film companies throughout her discouraging day. Images, symbolic of her frame of mind and physical condition, are touched in lightly. Sitting on the side of her bed, she stares at the veins of her fat legs. On the street, when a cat without a tail laps spilled milk, it gives her a peculiar feeling. After her final rejection she walks through the cold, away from the Bitter Orange Company and discards an application form on which she can check none of the skills needed. Resting on a bench in Square Gardens, she hopes someone feeds the sparrows, for which she has nothing. The added description of her walk past male clients and waiters in the Café de Madrid, is a kind of crescendo, as she goes to a table where she knows she will be slyly solicited for prostitution. When "The Common Round" has become "Pictures," Mansfield has learned how to turn interior monologue into a short story. In rewriting this work and *The Aloe,* she has learned what to add and what to delete. She is ready to write "Mr. Reginald Peacock's Day" and "Je ne Parle pas Français."

Two more stories may have been written after "Prelude" was completed. "Feuille d'Album" also foreshadows "Je ne Parle pas" by opening the account of a sensitive young man from the distanced viewpoint of a superficial woman, who seems to be telling the story. When she is interrupted by a question from an auditor, the viewpoint becomes multiple through such transitions as "Someone else decided that he ought to fall in love" and " 'What the poor boy really wants is thoroughly rousing,' said a third" (325). The omniscient author intrudes, removing the narrative from "those tender women," and then melts into the viewpoint of the central character himself. The shifts are managed with an ease that is also evident in "Prelude."

The last and most successful of the *New Age* group, "A Dill Pickle," is contained in the mind of Vera until the end, when she has left the scene and the author must finish. From the conversational recollections of the man and woman who meet by chance after a separation of six years and from her interior monologue the reader infers Vera's lonely need for, yet dissatisfaction with, this man. Though the reader may conclude that her criteria were in some points superficial, after she goes, the man's actions confirm her impressions of his parsimony and insensitivity:

> She had gone. He sat there, thunder-struck, astounded beyond words. . . . [Mansfield's ellipsis] And then he asked the waitress for his bill.
> "But the cream has not been touched," he said. "Please do not charge me for it." (337).

This closing with an omniscient viewpoint has almost resulted in the double-plotted effect which emerges in "Je ne Parle pas," for it thus completes an implicit story of the past as well as the immediate account of the present.

Mingled with this context of technical experiment was a clarification of attitude. For the *New Age* the stories were necessarily caustic, but upon "Prelude," as upon "Something Childish" and "An Indiscreet Journey," no editorial policy was imposed. Still, the satire was not artificial. Mansfield was fastidious. She could be offended by black caps or stinginess, and superficial, selfish responses to the war continued to dishearten her when she became a literary critic for the *Athenaeum*.[4] There was a link between the bitter mockery and the flashes of compassion, which now grew from the sudden insight of "Bains Turcs" to the extended expression of understanding that is "Prelude." During the writing of "Je ne Parle pas," in a letter of 3 February 1918, Mansfield defined the impulses which more or less classify her writing:

> Ive two "kick offs" in the writing game. *One* is joy—real joy—the thing that made me write when we lived at Pauline [she worked on *The Aloe* there]. . . . Then something delicate and lovely seems to open before my eyes, like a flower without thought of a frost or a cold breath—knowing that all about it is warm and tender and "steady." And *that* I try, ever so humbly to express.
> The other "kick off" is my old original one, and (had I not known love) it would have been my all. Not hate or destruction . . . but an *extremely* deep sense of hopelessness—of everything doomed to disaster—almost wilfully, stupidly—like the almond tree and "pas de nougat pour le noël" . . . *a cry against corruption.* (*Letters,* 2:54)

In "Something Childish" and in "An Indiscreet Journey" she had learned through a studied flow of image and paradoxical observation to render implicit in an apparently simple story a complex statement. Each story, in different ways, combined the attitudes Mansfield described as separate, for each is a cry against the failure or destruction of joy. The failure of young love and the irrational destiny of the forlorn yet comic soldier who sometimes looks like a saint are corruptions to be lamented like the withering of the almond blossom—changes from goodness, beauty, and joy to some lesser state, a falling off, a decay, death—a preoccupation as her health fails. "Prelude," though she asserts that she tried there to express joy, is everywhere fraught with negative awareness.

The title *The Aloe,* the first version of "Prelude," draws attention instructively to the dominant image of the story. The child Kezia, exploring the grounds of her new home, wanders away from a "tangle of tall dark trees and strange bushes" on "the frightening side, and no garden at all" to the other side of the drive, where she finds a "deeper and deeper tangle of flowers" (239).

In bloom are camellias, syringa, many varieties of roses, fairy bells, geraniums, verbena, lavender, pelagoniums, mignonette, pansies, daisies, red-hot pokers, and sunflowers. The enumeration conveys her pleasure. But as she turns toward the house, she sees an unknown plant, symbolically located on the "island" which divided the drive into its two arms of opposing character: "Nothing grew on the top [of the island] except one huge plant with thick, grey-green, thorny leaves, and out of the middle there sprang up a tall stout stem. Some of the leaves of the plant were so old that they curled up in the air no longer; they turned back, they were split and broken; some of them lay flat and withered on the ground" (240).

Significantly cut from "Prelude" is the only affirmative sentence in the description. *The Aloe* reads at this point: "[B]ut the fresh leaves curled up into the air with their spiked edges; some of them looked as though they had been painted with broad bands of yellow."[5] Nothing fresh or bright remains in the final version. As Linda Burnell, in answer to her daughter Kezia's question, looks at the plant, she sees "its cruel leaves and fleshy stem. High above them, as though becalmed in the air, and yet holding so fast to the earth it grew from, it might have had claws instead of roots. The curving leaves seemed to be hiding something; the blind stem cut into the air as if no wind could ever shake it."

And Kezia learns that it flowers rarely, at hundred-years intervals (239–40). This is the only moment of kinship between the remote mother and her daughter, as they both sense the menace of the plant. Neither knows the likeness of the other's awareness, yet it is as though each sees here the image of her secret fear: "IT" waiting for Kezia in the silent empty house they have just moved from, "THEY" filling Linda's rooms with threatening anticipation, smiling "their sly secret smile" (234).[6]

In the evening Linda's mother, Mrs. Fairfield, the affirmative and ordering force of the family, discovers buds on the aloe. Linda agrees that the plant is in bud and tells her mother, "I am sure I shall remember it long after I've forgotten all the other things." She has envisioned the aloe as a ship, and herself being quickly rowed away on it, a "more real . . . dream . . . than that they should go back to the house," which holds her sleeping children, Stanley [Linda's husband] and Beryl [her sister] (257). The aloe serves here to reinforce the recurrent motif of Linda's desire to escape. Her morning vision had shown her "in a little buggy, driving away from everybody and not even waving," very much the way she had left Kezia and Lottie, "cast them off," the day before. Again Mansfield increases the negative weight of the symbol, by removing in her final draft all association of Mrs. Fairfield with that flight.[7]

As Linda looks at the aloe, metaphorically the flowering occurs, but it is a flowering of realization in her own mind: "From below she could see the long sharp thorns that edged the aloe leaves, and at the sight of them her heart grew hard. . . . [Mansfield's ellipsis] She particularly liked the long sharp thorns. . . . Nobody would dare to come near the ship or to follow after." As her mind follows the train of thought unleashed by her response to the aloe, she recognizes her hatred, despite "all her love and respect and admiration," of Stanley: "It had never been so plain to her as it was at this moment. There were all her feelings for him, sharp and defined, one as true as the other. And there was this other, this hatred, just as real as the rest" (258).

As she came to this knowledge, yielding to the destructive violence of the aloe, she "snatched her hand from mother's arm." Her gesture underlines the story's polarities: serenity, goodness, order, manifest in every action and word of Mrs. Fairfield, and the ominous menace implicit in the silent, unmoving appearance of the aloe. Between their rival claims waver Linda and Kezia, the major characters of the story. Linda concludes negatively, finding life absurd, her desire to live a mania, and the future promising more of what she has, more of what she does not want: children, money, and gardens "with whole fleets of aloes in them" (258). The menace will intensify.

Biographers have mistakenly regarded Linda as an antagonistic portrait of Mansfield's mother. But in *The Aloe* the characterization is sympathetic. Linda's indifference to the children is expressed as jokes, one a threat to send them to an orphanage. When Stanley exercises, "she leaned toward him laughing." The first mention of her desire to run away from house and family she dismisses as "a silly thought" (*Aloe,* 24, 23). Deleting such details for "Prelude" renders her more serious and less frightening to the children. Her accommodation of Stanley is generous in light of her fear of his intense sexuality and of childbirth. It also continues the *German Pension* theme that women suffer in the marital bed and in bearing children.

With Kezia the conclusion is less clear, for Kezia's consciousness is less mature, less fixed than her mother's. The two are parallel not only in their fears and in their feeling for the aloe but, of course, in their need for Mrs. Fairfield, the only answer to that menace. Linda clearly recognizes that order is the adjunct of her mother. Finding her in the kitchen, where under her hand "everything . . . had become part of a series of patterns," Linda comments, "It says 'mother' all over; everything is in pairs." And watching her, Linda is aware of her own need: "There was something comforting in the sight of her that Linda felt she could never do without" (237–38). But waking that morning, Linda had seen the orderliness of the bedroom, in which "all the furniture had found a place—" and she had rejected it. "[S]he wished that she was going away from this house, too" (232).

Kezia is too young to think about her relationship to her grandmother, but in the two days of "Prelude" she turns often to the comfort of this orderly woman. It is the grandmother she wishes to kiss good-bye, when she and little sister Lottie are left behind with the unmoved furniture. Characteristically, in this scene the grandmother has settled on the plan of leaving the children with Mrs. Samuel Josephs, while Linda only associates them whimsically with "the tables and chairs standing on their heads on the front lawn. How absurd they looked! Either they ought to be the other way up, or Lottie and Kezia ought to stand on their heads, too" (220). From "How absurd. . . ." this passage was added in revision, clearly to emphasize Linda's mocking sense of humor and to anticipate her final view of life.

Kezia explores disorder but usually turns away from it. She pokes in the rubbish left in her family's old house and knows there will be none left in her grandmother's room. She wanders away from or resists the games devised by her older sister, but even in her recalcitrance she behaves with the orderly habit of Mrs. Fairfield: "She began to lay the cloth on a pink garden seat. In front of each person she put two geranium leaf plates, a pine needle fork and a twig knife. There were three daisy heads on a laurel leaf for poached eggs, some slices of fuchia petal cold beef, some lovely little rissoles made of earth and water and dandelion seeds, and the chocolate custard which she decided to serve in the pawa shell she had cooked it in" (246). These miniature and imaginative precisions are akin to the matchbox surprise she plans to make for her grandmother.

Sometimes disorder discomfits her. The empty house grew frightening. She looked at the bull that Linda airily thought had tossed her, but she "had not liked the bull frightfully, so she had walked away" (238). In the garden she turned from the dark side of strange bushes where the paths were ill-kept to the side where the paths had box edges and the flowers were known. Amid this pleasant beauty she thought of her grandmother.

For Kezia the most intense conflict of order with the menace occurs in the beheading of the duck: "[Pat] put down the body and it began to waddle—with only a long spurt of blood where the head had been; it began to pad away without a sound towards the steep bank that led to the stream. . . . [Mansfield's ellipsis]" (251).

Even in death the nervous system mysteriously attempts the patterned behavior of life. At that Kezia cries out for the restoration of order: "Put head back! Put head back!" For a moment she is violent in her grief. Then, like Linda and Beryl, she is diverted, in this case by the strangeness of Pat's gold earrings. But she is not completely consoled. Deleted from "Prelude" is the *Aloe* comment "[S]he quite forgot about the duck" (*Aloe,* 57). She did *not* forget. Remaining in "Prelude" is Kezia's veiled rebuke: "Do they come on and off?" she asks (252). The removal of an earring lacks the finality of the duck's reluctant and horrifying death. Linda will turn from her rejection of life, brought on by the sight of the cruel aloe, to the scent of verbena, the beauty of camellia trees, and her mother's companionship.

But if there is a direction in the author's attitude it is negative. The duck's head cannot be put back. Linda does, despite her love, hate Stanley, fear childbearing, prefer the aloe as a metaphoric ship which will carry her away and defend her from pursuit. Order to her mother involves an acceptance of life—its work, its pain, its Stanleys. Mrs. Fairfield can make it all into something of calm beauty, but this order, Linda feels, is killing her; from the productive life of Stanley and her mother she flees, in her indifference, to aloofness, even to mockery of their realities: food, economy, well-arranged kitchens, children, sexual relations. She would like to run away in fact as well as in imagination.

The last word is not Mrs. Fairfield's, as, unaware of Linda's vision of the aloe, she thinks of turning the fruit into jam. Final emphasis lies in the implications of the last scene, that between Beryl and Kezia. Throughout much of the story Beryl has helped with the moving, "slaved" toward the creation of order in the house. But her work has not been like the creative work of her mother and Kezia. Beryl is sullen, resents the move to the country, is mean in her treatment of the children. She deplores Stanley's taste and his demands, yet because the pose pleases her, probably as a contrast to her indifferent older sister, she flirts with him over the cribbage board. In the final scene, in which she is writing a letter, she becomes disgusted with herself and reviews her behavior:

> "I know that I am silly and spiteful and vain; I'm always acting a part. I'm never my real self for a moment."
> . . . .
> If she had been happy and leading her own life, her false life would cease to be. She saw the real Beryl—a shadow. . . . a shadow. Faint and unsubstantial she shone. What was there of her except the radiance? And for what tiny moments she was really she. . . . At those times she had felt: "Life is rich and mysterious and good, and I am rich and mysterious and good, too." . . . Was there ever the time when I did not have a false self? (262)

Two long omissions from *The Aloe* passage of self-analysis place the emphasis on Beryl's inability to improve. In one her false self is becoming more and more dominant (*Aloe,* 73–74). In the other she imagines the repeated scene of Nan Pym brushing her hair; though this repels Beryl, she allows it to continue (*Aloe,* 75–76). Deleting these leaves the "Prelude" emphasis on Beryl's "radiance" and her affirmation of her self as "rich and mysterious and good" (262).

This is Beryl's cry against corruption, and the answer seems to appear in Kezia's entrance. Kezia brings a call to lunch and the news that father has brought a man home. She carries a cat. When Beryl has gone, Kezia meddles with things not her own. She sets the top of Beryl's cream jar upon the cat's ear. The cat falls and with it the cream jar lid.

> [It] flew through the air and rolled like a penny in a round on the linoleum—and did not break.
> But for Kezia it had broken the moment it flew through the air, and she picked it up, hot all over, and put it back on the dressing table.
> The she tip-toed away, far too quickly and airily. . . . (263)

So Kezia too is a pretender and, for the moment, false. Though it is a child's defensive, harmless pretense, the gesture answers Beryl's question: "[W]as there ever a time when I did not have a false self?"

Ending here, "Prelude" portrays four stages of womanhood. Kezia, the child, reaches for the order and serenity of her grandmother, who draws strength from her commitment to practical reality. The adolescent Beryl would like to be real but finds herself almost entirely false. Her romantic dreams of courtship by a lover with money contrast with Linda's appraisal as a woman who has secured love, marriage, and security but finds realistic disadvantages in these objectives. For Kezia and Beryl, the two days of the story describe a prelude, a beginning, but for Linda the game is nearly up. Her rejection of domesticity is made even more conclusive in that she, unlike Beryl, knows her mother's worth. Perhaps Beryl and Kezia can attain the affirmative state of Mrs. Fairfield. But Kezia's easy distraction from her protest at the duck's death, her final stealthy posture, the predominant falsity of Beryl, and above all, the crucial significance of the aloe leave the final emphasis on the passing of innocence and on the victory, in the withering blossom, of corruption.

" 'What form it is?' you ask," Mansfield wrote to Dorothy Brett, the October after she had finished the revision.

> Ah, Brett, it's so difficult to say. As far as I know, it's more or less my own invention. And how have I shaped it? . . . I always remember feeling that this little island [New Zealand] has dipped back into the dark blue sea during the night only to rise again at beam of day, all hung with bright spangles and glittering drops. . . . I tried to catch that moment— with something of its sparkle and flavour. And just as on those mornings white milky mists rise and uncover some beauty, then smother it again and then again disclose it, I tried to lift that mist from my people, and let them be seen and then to hide them again. . . ." (*Letters*, 1:331 Mansfield's ellipsis).

The innovation lies in letting the story unfold in the immediacy of many consciousnesses, rendered by the self-effacing projection of the omniscient author. Interpretation of the sort continually imposed upon nearly every act of his characters by the all-knowing, distant Chekhov is avoided. The reader learns the thoughts and feelings of the characters only from their own responses. No characterization is adulterated by dependence on another. The reader, as with a Chekhov story, is left to infer the final meaning; however, Mansfield compels her reader to work more immediately upon the data. As in a poem, she holds the audience poised upon the turns of each mind, so that as participants, they develop and create the larger complex: the characters' and their own interwoven responses, which, for the careful reader, will be something near that experience toward which the author's control has led. This involvement of the reader in multiple viewpoints, so easily overlapped that it is sometimes difficult in the later stories to specify when the change from one to another occurred, is Mansfield's most influential contribution to the modern short story.

Though *The Aloe* began as autobiographical memory, that self-indulgence has been consistently edited out of "Prelude." Gone are New Zealand geography and place-names, detailed description of the Karori house and grounds, the account of Kezia/Mansfield's birth, and the entire scene and character of "Mrs. Trout" (based on Mansfield's aunt). With many slight verbal changes the old Paterian "prettiness" has also disappeared. Mansfield has worked through to the objectivity she desired as an artist. No longer the naive, intrusive narrator of *In a German Pension,* she has learned her craft. Unlike many of her later critics and biographers, she now knows the difference between biography and fiction.[8]

In the early months of 1916 at Bandol, while Mansfield was at work on *The Aloe,* Murry wrote his first book of literary criticism, *Fyodor Dostoyevsky.* Mansfield's *Journal* (109–112) indicates, as would be expected, that she took an interest in the study. When she sent Murry the first part of "Je ne Parle pas Français," he wrote excitedly, "[M]y sensation is like that which I had when I read Dostoevsky's *Letters from the Underworld. . . .* it's utterly unlike any sensation I have ever yet had from any writing of yours, or any writing at all except D's " (*Letters btwn,* 112). She herself could only exclaim, "I read the fair copy just now and couldn't think where the devil I had got the bloody thing from—I can't even now" (*Letters,* 2:56). But in the broadest outline, the story does have a kinship in tone, characterization, and form to Dostoyevsky's short novel. In the Russian work an egotistical man, part sadist, part masochist, with literary pretensions, reveals in first person his own loathsome nature. Within the account of his life he includes, because the snow is falling, a rather lengthy story called "A propos of the Wet Snow." This recollection of an earlier experience in his life occupies two-thirds of the novel, which ends immediately upon the end of the anecdote.

The shape of "Je ne Parle pas" is similar, but it has been concentrated in a short story. A greater change is that Raoul Duquette, the encompassing narrator, by acting as a narrator on the fringe of one story, paradoxically tells two other stories of himself. The crisis of the first is the failure of Dick Harmon to remain in France with Mouse after their elopement. Raoul Duquette's echoic rejection only confirms his exposé of his character and provides him with a point of departure for the tale of his "grand moment." That he encircles it with a third story, an apparently irrelevant account of himself, conveys simultaneously his sterile effeminacy and his overweening self-esteem. To him the point of major significance is not that Mouse has been left desolate in Paris but that he, who abandoned her after knowing fully her helplessness, can at the recollection experience "such an intensity of feeling so . . . purely (354; Mansfield's ellipsis)." Nonetheless, this view, his mannered style, and the arrangement of materials are calculated more importantly to damn him than to lament the fate of Mouse. The form of the story serves to engulf Mouse in the horror that is the narrator's character.

The arrangement of the encircling story is deceptively simple; it is based on the raising of curiosity in the reader and then, after a small delay in which character and setting are exposed, satisfying that curiosity. "I do not know why I have such a fancy for this little café"—the opening sentence—calls for a description of the "dirty and sad, sad" place and its clientele, with a "long and rather far-fetched digression" in which the reader is told that Duquette does not believe in the human soul, and infers from his style that he is artificial and self-conscious. The key passage is slyly buried in the digression, when the narrator images himself as a customs official examining the portmanteaus, his metaphor for people, "packed with certain things. . . ." 'Have you anything to declare?' he asks: And the moment of hesitation as to whether I am going to be fooled just before I chalk that squiggle, and then the other moment of hesitation just after, as to whether I have been, are perhaps the two most thrilling instants in life (350–51). This describes his position with regard to Dick and Mouse—his avid, dehumanized interest in their feelings as they act out their failure. But it relates also to his veiled attitude toward Dick. He has been fooled, not by Dick but by his own egotistical assumption and desire during their first encounter, when he believed Dick was erotically attracted to him. Dick's abrupt, casual departure then angered Duquette, who anticipates vengeance when Dick returns with Mouse. When Dick deserts Mouse, Duquette rejoices: "I was even—more than even with my Englishman" (375).

After this much exposition the reader learns that Duquette likes the café because he experienced there a moment of intense feeling. There is another delay, rich with self-exposure, as the preparation for the moment is described; then he notices on a blotting paper seized to record a "rather nice . . . bit about the Virgin" "that stupid, stale little phrase: *Je ne parle pas français*" (353). At which the moment occurs:

> How can I describe it? I didn't think of anything. I didn't even cry out to myself. Just for one moment I was not. I was Agony, Agony, Agony.
>
> Then it passed, and the very second after I was thinking: "Good God! Am I capable of feeling as strongly as that? (354).

As the reader wonders about the cause of the moment, Duquette reveals that he has "made it a rule of [his] life never to regret and never to look back," but even as he writes this, his "other self has been chasing up and down out in the dark there" looking unsuccessfully "like a lost dog" for a girl named Mouse (355). With that much of a promise to lure him, the reader is led through several more pages of Duquette autobiography and finally to the story of the attempted elopement of Mouse and Dick. The high-flown description of his "moment" early in the story, followed by the steady revelation of his composed enjoyment of suffering, results in a deterioration of the reader's opinion. In the end the narrator says, "Of course you know what to expect (376). So at last the cause of the moment is known. He abandoned Mouse, but he does remember her. And that is the story of his banality, by which ironically he sets out to demonstrate that he is "first-rate."

That his proof rests upon his response to the phrase which most completely expressed to him Mouse's helplessness in Paris, is the peak of his insensitivity. Her last words to Duquette, as she accepted his offer of help, were "It makes things rather difficult because . . . *je ne parle pas français*" (376). And Duquette insistently labors the effect on him of that remark. Having exposed his callousness, his perverted childhood, and his career as gigolo, and imaged himself as a dog and a woman, he reveals that this event is his only compensation for a latent lack of self-respect: "If you think what I've written is merely superficial and impudent and cheap you're wrong. I'll admit it does sound so, but then it is not at all. If it were, how could I have experienced what I did when I read that stale little phrase written in green ink, in the writing-pad? That proves there's more in me and that I really am important, doesn't it?" (358).

How perfectly Mansfield has caught Murry's character: his indecisiveness, his dependence on her courage, but most particularly, when he has failed another, his solipsistic absorption in his own desolation rather than that of his victim. Always self-regarding and obtusely shameless in his self-exposure, Murry wrote 36 pages *(B2W,* 137–73) on his abortive affair of 1911 with the Parisian seamstress Margueritte. By his account he yielded to her sexual advances so she would stop crying, and lacking courage to "[p]art from her [he] simply ran away," having decided it was "far better to let her think" it was to return to his mother, which, in fact, he did. Deceitfully he promised to come back. When he left her at the railroad station he "knew what the anguish of love could be" and, still pained nearly 25 years later, obligingly wrote a page on that topic. He concluded his lament, "Even today, fantastic though it sounds, the thought that there was once a moment when it was uncertain, when it was not a fixed and inexorable destiny [note that it wasn't Murry's fault!] that I should never see her again, unmans me."

Mansfield's opening section of "Je ne Parle pas français" seems prescient, but she is only recording, in a caustic context, Murry's own manner. When "the moment" occurs, Duquette asserts, "I was Agony, Agony, Agony. . . . And up I puffed and puffed . . . with 'After all I must be first rate. No second-rate mind could have experienced such an intensity of feeling so . . . purely' " (354; final ellipsis Mansfield's). While Mansfield was writing the story, Murry apologetically wrote her, excusing his insentient responses: "[I]t must be confessed that I am rather a second rate affair" *(Letters btwn.,* 105). His own anguish is also the primary concern of Dick Harmon in his self-indulgent farewell note to Mouse. He finds his indecision "unspeakably awful." He is too tired to think, especially of Mouse's position. He urges her not to be frightened: "I can't bear—but no more of that," he writes. Nor will be able to bear her letters, "the sight of your spidery handwriting" (374–75). Like Murry, he is running home to Mother.[9]

Toward the end of the story, Duquette describes his indecision: "I never went near the place again. . . . Naturally I intended to. Started out—got to the door—wrote and tore up letters—did all those things. But I simply could not make the final effort (376–77). Compare Murry's 1911 return to Paris: "[A]fter twenty-four hours of waiting in a Paris hotel to find the courage to meet her, I fled to England. . . . [F]or weeks an ashy sense of degradation invaded me—a feeling that . . . I was being given over to decay and corruption" *(B2W,* 173).

Though as the story was finally written the misled, despicable Duquette tells it, Newberry Library Mansfield Papers reveal that he was not originally conceived as the narrator. Box I.27 is the earlier draft, written in Mansfield's rapid, difficult composing hand, with corrections made in her careful copying hand, the hand of Box I.26.[10] The first draft has no title, and the titular phrase discovered on the blotting paper is "I don't speak English," crossed out later when the copying hand wrote above, "Je ne parle pas français." Near the end of the next section, after many corrections to arrive at the sermon against "wallowing in regret," which is "fatal to art" and a poverty "Art can't and won't stand" (354–55), the composing Mansfield wrote twice, "I do not speak English."

Clearly in the original concept Mouse was French and the narrator was English. What story had Mansfield begun to tell? Obviously Murry's own, his adventure of 1911, with a commentary on the self-indulgent, lachrymose manner of his telling. Mansfield deplored that manner. In a letter of the previous July she had written of his *Times Literary Supplement* article on Leon Bloy, "I feel that you are going to uncover yourself and quiver. . . . You seem to abase yourself. . . . Its perfectly natural to you I know, but oh my God, dont do it. . . . I am ashamed that you should speak so" *(Letters,* 1:318).

The difficulty in composing the "wallowing in regret" passage, followed by more disgust as the narrator images himself as a dog, must have alerted Mansfield to the likelihood that by exposing Murry and revealing her contempt through an account of Dick Harmon's betraying cowardice, she would endanger a relationship which she continued to value. Or perhaps it was compassion that decided her to spare him. In any case she had only to change the English phrase to French, nothing else of what she had written, for she had not yet named the narrator or begun his autobiographical remarks.

The next section begins, "My name is Raoul Duquette." Art benefits, as the change in intent results in more complex characterization and the intricate structuring of three interwoven stories. The change also veils the message to Murry, overbalancing it by allusions to Carco. Dick Harmon's abandonment of Mouse becomes minor compared with Duquette's decadent luxuriance as he dwells sadistically on his multiple villainies. His treatment of Mouse appears to be an aspect of his revenge on Dick Harmon.

Duquette has given the impression throughout his account that Mouse was left helpless in Paris, but nothing in his characterization suggests that his judgment is trustworthy. In fact, Mansfield has not portrayed Mouse as a victim. From her first appearance in the story, she has behaved competently. She enters the railroad scene taking care of the baggage, while the physically able Harmon flutters in nervous disarray. She tells him what to do, to help the porter, and where the luggage should be placed. She orders tea. And though she has denied it, she does speak *French*. "Of course she does," Harmon assures Duquette. And when she orders tea "with her quaint clipped English accent" (370), the French narrator, an unlikely appraiser of *English* dialects, can only be referring to her pronunciation of his own French language.

Mouse has anticipated Harmon's betrayal from the beginning. Though she weeps at Harmon's letter, her face remains calm, the tears brief. "I knew it all the time," she says, and denounces her continuing hope as stupid (375). She will make no attempt to see him again.

And she does have £20, on which, in 1918 Paris, Mansfield knew she could live for two months or more.[11] As Mansfield's *persona*, Mouse had to be a survivor.

Besides the implication of Duquette's failure to act and the many details of his own self-description, the motif of a song runs through the story to provide a further comment. It is Dick's English song about a homeless man looking for dinner. The time of two of the stories Duquette tells—the enveloping story and the story of the moment—is afternoon. In each the occasion for entering the café is that he "was drifting along, either going home or not going home." The wide variety of his experiences with women has been stated as well as that they always have "made the first advances." The proprietress of the café he favors is described as restless, as hopelessly pretending to look for someone she knows will not come. The story ends:

> I must go. I must go. I reach down my coat and hat. Madame knows me. "You haven't dined yet?" she smiles.
> "No, not yet, Madame." (377)

There is an implication here that this hungry, hollow man, who has fed so avidly on the sorrows of Mouse and of Dick Harmon, will continue his parasitic ventures in another meal, feasting this time on the less moving loneliness of Madame.

In letters of February 1920 Mansfield and Murry debated Michael Sadleir's prudish censorship for the Constable edition of *Bliss and Other Stories*. The omitted text is unnecessary but confirms the sexual focus of Duquette's musings. Murry had included them in his Heron Press edition of 1920:

> I'd rather like to dine with her. Even to sleep with her afterwards. Would she be pale like that all over?

But no. She'd have large moles. They go with that kind of skin. I can't bear them. They remind me somehow, disgustingly, of large mushrooms.

Also censored were references to prostitutes and virgins and greater specificity when the Negress seduced the child Duquette: "And then with a soft growl she tore open her bodice and put me to her."[12]

The form of this story was very important to Katherine Mansfield. "I've got to reconstruct everything" was her first appraisal. She never repeated it quite so elaborately. "A Married Man's Story," according to Murry's note, begun in May when she wrote, "I have started working—another member of the Je ne Parle pas family, I fondly dream—"(*Letters,* 2:188), is similar in shape, but it was not finished. The only finished story close in form is "Poison," a much briefer incident enclosing the narrator's story of a youthful experience in his own, older viewpoint.

The intricacy of structure of "Je ne Parle pas Français" did not matter so much as the utter removal of author, the very full realization of character and scene solely through a single point of view, and the free shifts in time made possible through that limitation. Beginning with "Bliss," many of the stories told from the viewpoint of a third-person narrator take on, with an increase in subtlety, this aspect of the form of "Je ne Parle pas." Others continue the multipersonal discoveries of "Prelude," with an effaced omniscient author moving among several points of view. In either case time is dealt with very freely through the exploitation of interior monologue, and meaning remains implicit in a paradoxical interplay of gesture, thought, and image.

Now the craft was found, and the depths of the consciousness so deeply plumbed that Murry, in his letter about "Je ne Parle pas," declared such a practice dangerous. Five years remained for the artist to convey her vision. She believed she had discovered its substance and the method. Her conviction and passion are evident in a letter of 16 November 1919:

> Now [after the war] we know ourselves for what we are. In a way it's a tragic knowledge—it's as though, even while we live again, we face death. But *through Life*: that's the point. We see death in life as we see death in a flower that is fresh unfolded. Our hymn is to the flower's beauty—we would make that beauty immortal because we *know*.
>
> . . . .
>
> I mean 'deserts of vast eternity.' But . . . I couldn't tell anybody *bang out* about those deserts—They are my secret. I might write about a boy eat-

ing strawberries or a woman combing her hair on a windy morning, &
that is the only way I can ever mention them. But they *must* be there.
Nothing less will do. (*Letters*, 3:97–98)

She would write out to the end her perceptions of beauty and her cry
against its corruption.

Chapter Five
Trains of Thought

"Je ne Parle pas" was scarcely finished when Mansfield dreamed and immediately wrote the short story "Sun and Moon." "It was very light" (*Letters,* 2:66), she wrote Murry, but the cry against corruption was nonetheless there. When five-year-old Sun sees the little ice cream house "broken—broken and half melted away," the offer of sweets does not appease him. He wails loudly and declares this passing of prettiness "horrid." Within two weeks of the composition, Mansfield was beginning to disavow it. "Would the Nation publish Sun and Moon?" she asked Murry. "If they publish that rubbish by Stephens I think they might" (*Letters,* 2:88). Nearly two years later: "No, Boge [pet name for Murry], dont send A. & L. [*Arts and Letters*] Sun and Moon if you don't mind. (1) Theyd not publish it (2) I feel far away from it" (*Letters,* 3:147). And on 27 September 1920: "Even though I'm poor as a Mouse don't publish Sun and Moon." But Murry, then editor of the *Athenaeum,* probably had the type set by then, for the story appeared on 1 October.

Mansfield wrote stories about children throughout her career, always with singular insight into their psychology. Perhaps because the material came easily as the result of dreams or of a capacity for total recall, she did not seem to value them highly. "My serious stories won't ever bring me anything but my 'child' stories ought to and my light ones, once I find a place," she told Murry in February 1918 (*Letters,* 2:75). She could not know then that she would write only three more " 'child' stories": "See—Saw," scarcely a sketch; the trivial "Sixpence"; and the very wonderful "A Doll's House," so intriguingly foreseen in "Sun and Moon."

The anxiety dream behind "Sun and Moon" reflects again Mansfield's intuitive awareness that Murry and their desire for a home together— the Heron, now turning into an Elephant[1]—will crumble. But the story is not a simple recounting of the dream. It has been solidified with recollections of childhood, paralleled in "Prelude" and in stories not yet written.

Dreamers usually identify with the protagonist of the dream. That Mansfield did so with the little boy Sun is evidenced in MP, Notebook 5, written in her first-draft composing hand with corrections inserted. The fourth paragraph opens, "They kept out of her way—at any rate Moon did." Moon, being the little girl, is corrected to Sun. Then the veiled autobiographical story of childish sibling rivalry, which dominates the story, begins. Unlike Moon, Sun is too heavy to toss into the air and is mocked for his weight by—add insult to injury—a fat man. The mark of rejection which he hates is "being sent stumping back to the nursery," exactly as he will end the story.

To the motif of fatness, for which the real, young Kathleen was criticized, are added other observations of the less favored child: Sun resents Moon's imitative laughter at his naive question, "Are people going to eat the food?" (380) Dressed up for display at his parents' party, he minds not being noticed while Moon is admired. And she pretends innocence after pulling the tablecloth away from him when they eat.

Parallels with other stories confirm the persistence of Mansfield's memory-motifs. The upside-down chairs which provide an early joke in "Prelude" open "Sun and Moon." The same indifferent mother thrusts the children aside. The festive party preparations, even to having a preliminary taste of a confection in the kitchen, will be repeated by older youngsters in "The Garden Party." The admired little ice cream house will solidify in "The Doll's House." Sun dreams of a little man with gray whiskers who liked the house the best of all the elegant party food. Focusing down to a minute detail Sun has admired, the little man, much as "our Els" would, asks, "Seen the nut?"—the tiny door handle (382). The final blow that leads to Sun's outcry occurs when his resented sister Moon "picked [the nut] out of the door and scrunched it up, biting hard" (383). The sister is callously and greedily complicit with the adults in the destruction of beauty.[2]

Murry misreads, solipsistically, as usual. "It's so damned true of us now," he writes. "These people . . . think we can feel delight in ice houses when the roof has been pushed in. . . . Save that we walk away hand in hand . . . it's all true". He has not noticed the antagonism between the two children. A few days later he makes that even clearer. He writes, " 'Sun and Moon' were really tinies. His tragedy would be put right. But Mouse and Dick, they were too much like us" (*Letters btwn.,* 120, 124).

The stories have left Murry uncomfortable. At least unconsciously he knows that in both "Sun and Moon" and "Je ne Parle pas Français" Mansfield is writing about his betrayals of Marguerrite and of herself.[3] The "child" story comes peculiarly closer, involving as it does the destruction of a house—their impossible dream of the Heron. Acknowledging none of this, Murry continues to reassure himself: "If they had been exactly like it wouldn't have upset me because I know we're alright. But they were different." Did Mansfield take it as ironic that he ended, "My eye is better. . . . I'll have to get some more glasses"? (*Letters btwn.,* 124). She must have hoped that he would get the message. Her letter about the dream had ended with this clue: "Our home is a cottage with a gold roof and silver windows" (*Letters,* 2:67).

At the other extreme were her satirical views of the pseudoartistic life of artists and the hangers-on of artistic life. This, indeed, was the world she could endure no more easily than she had submitted to the world of the German pension. But her pen had grown subtler. Moving through a few hours of a day or, at the most, a weekend, she let these people expose themselves. In the dialogue or interior monologues of "Psychology," "Revelations," and "A Dill Pickle" she needed only a brief encounter to delineate shallowness.

In "Mr. Reginald Peacock's Day" it took just that long. The consciousness of this affected singing teacher reveals a man hypersensitive to his own comfort. His many female students and the idle, wealthy women who hear his concerts gush adulation. But his wife manages the household and their young son only for his convenience. Though he does not acknowledge it, his petulant selfishness has deprived her of the servant he rebukes her for not having. Throughout the day, as he teaches and dines with affable ladies, he repeats to any advance, "Dear lady, I should be only too charmed." At the end of his very successful day, moved by the condescension and champagne of a noble lord, he would like to tell his wife of his triumphs. But he is trapped by his own artificiality and can utter only the empty phrase he reserves for the other ladies. The ironic summation of his behavior is found in an adoring lady's letter—"You are teaching the world to escape from life" (387, 392). The story, told entirely from Peacock's viewpoint, describes the utter misogyny of the vain artist, contemptuous of his servant-wife and condescending to his admirers, naturally all of them women. Could it be for that very reason that Peacock is allowed to muse, in his drunken stagger home, "I could have any one I liked by lifting a finger" (392)?[4]

Rosemary Fell, the smart, affluent, but insincere young woman of "A Cup of Tea," damns herself, like Raoul Duquette, through avidity for an exciting experience which feeds on another's misery. The story is viewed by an omniscient narrator who stylistically adopts a persona very close to that of Rosemary herself. The voice of the opening paragraph is malicious: "Rosemary Fell was not exactly beautiful. No, you couldn't have called her beautiful. Pretty? Well, if you took her to pieces . . . But why be so cruel as to take anyone to pieces?" (584; Mansfield's ellipsis). When the narrator moves to a reflection of Rosemary's thinking, it is hard to tell the difference. Meeting a hungry girl on the street, Rosemary thinks, "It was like something out of a novel by Dostoyevsky, this meeting in the dusk. Supposing she took the girl home? What would happen? It would be thrilling" (586).

Rosemary is artificial, idle, insensitive. The contrast between the £5 she reduces to 3 as a gift to the penniless girl and the useless but pretty 28-guinea box she asks of her husband reveals her selfish materialism. But the final detail of her exposure dwells on her insecure vanity, the real reason for dismissing the young woman whom her husband called "astonishingly pretty." The words echo in Rosemary's mind as she finds money for the girl. Later she has "just done her hair, darkened her eyes a little, and put on her pearls," when she whispers to her husband, "Philip . . . am I pretty?" (590–91).

The malicious arrangement of data is augmented by the malicious tone of the narrator. It is as though such behavior deserves no compassion. The fallibility of the narrator's mood motivates the organization but does not call into question the facts of the case. The conception of the story has altered considerably from "The Dark Hollow" (*Scrapbook,* 34–44), a first study of similar relations between two women. In this early and unfinished draft the two are old schoolmates. The penniless one, however, instead of merely weeping, tells a false story of her hard life to the kind, generous friend who has determined to take her in. The shift of the needy girl to a lower social position may have controlled Mansfield's sympathy.[5] Though she often complained in her letters of the crudity and incompetence of servants and of other "inferiors," this illiberal sentiment she apparently feared might be snobbery. The final literary statements were always compassionate.

In "Marriage à la Mode" and in "Bliss" Mansfield moved to the condemnation of groups. Murry described these stories as "semi-sophisticated" failures. He felt that "the stupider *intelligentsia*" is the subject and that "the discordant combination of caricature with emotional pathos . . . spoils" them both.[6] But these discords in "Marriage" intensify the sense of William's puzzled, honest anguish when he is confronted by the falseness of Isabel and her crowd. In "Bliss" the fact that Bertha in her excited anticipation must await her climax and then see it turn to dust is well accompanied by the sterility of her guests. As doubtful as Murry's are Berkman's criticisms that "William's unhappy soliloquies . . . are scarce-

ly masculine" and that Bertha's "overwrought, gushing manner . . .
alienates sympathy" (*Berkman,* 180, 183). The intention of these effects,
however, deserves further examination.

When Mansfield chooses to portray an effeminate man, she selects for
him a characterizing diction and syntax. Raoul Duquette, Reginald
Peacock, Bobby Kane of "Marriage à la Mode," and Eddie Warren of
"Bliss" are all excessively articulate. *Charming* is not only the echoic word
of Peacock but frequently runs through the mind of Duquette. Eddie
Warren describes too many experiences as *dreadful,* and italics indicate
that the rhythms of his speech are those stereotypically stigmatized as
effeminate. His exaggerated description—"so wonderful," "deeply
true"—are paralleled by Duquette's "so exactly the gesture," "so tender,
so reassuring," "so amazingly in the picture," and by Bobby Kane's
"really look too divine" and "a perfect little ballet" (559 ff.). All are conscious of the images they present of themselves, ranging from delighted
admiration of white sock's to operatic gestures in the bathtub.

None of these stances are William's. He reads business papers and
meditates about the change in Isabel, but the language of his monologue
at its most poetic is "manly." His farthest flight is a memory of childhood: "The exquisite freshness of Isabel! When he had been a little boy,
it was his delight to run into the garden after a shower of rain and shake
the rose-bush over him. Isabel was that rose-bush, petal-soft, sparkling
and cool" (556). His conversation is laconic, inexpressive. Of his love letter there is quoted one straightforward sentence: "God forbid, my darling, that I should be a drag on your happiness" (563). It is just his
down-to-earth mien and his resulting inability to play a part among
Isabel's pretentious friends that causes his alienation. William is, in fact,
a rather neutral figure who wins sympathy only because the group which
causes his misery is cruel and tasteless. Greedy, idle, and dull, Isabel and
her friends reach a peak of bad taste in their mockery of William's letter.
That Isabel—even recognizing that the incident was "vile, odious,
abominable, vulgar" (564)—cannot reform completes the analysis of her
character and exposes it as William's greatest disaster.

Bertha Young is similar in aspiration to "high culture," but, unlike
Isabel, she is the betrayed, not the betrayer. In "Bliss" Mansfield inten-
tionally portrays Bertha's manner as "overwrought." She is, as Berkman
notes, hysterical and recognizes it herself as she begins to laugh at the end
of the first section of the story. Again and again through the evening
Bertha controls her rising laughter. Repeatedly it is clear that she is
attempting unsuccessfully to deceive herself. Concerning her guests her

self-deception is not immediately obvious: "They had people coming to dinner. The Norman Knights—a very sound couple . . . a young man, Eddie Warren, who had just published a little book of poems . . . and a 'find' of Bertha's called Pearl Fulton . . . Bertha had fallen in love with her, as she always did fall in love with beautiful women who had something strange about them" (340–41). But when the guests arrive, Mrs. Knight looks to Bertha "like a very intelligent monkey," and her mind pursues the image, dressing the woman in banana skins, pretending that she hoards nuts in her bodice and that she is cold without her red flannel jacket, typical monkey garb. The silent mockery mounts until "Bertha had to dig her nails into her hands—so as not to laugh too much." Mr. Knight's gestures with his monocle appear equally absurd to her. And conversation with Eddie must also be stifled to avoid rudeness. When he tells her that there is a moon, "[s]he wanted to cry: 'I am sure there is—often—often,' " and later she thinks of "poor dear Eddie's moon" (343, 346).

It is clear, then, that what Bertha tells herself and the responses she makes to stimuli within the story are in conflict. This is the key to what otherwise would be a badly controlled story. She is a treacherously fallible narrator. The contrast between deliberately verbalized attitude and attitude conveyed by gesture or unbidden feeling must be examined in order to grasp her dealings with Pearl Fulton and with her husband, Harry. It is very likely that her high excitement, which she interprets at first as "bliss" but soon calls "hysteria," has arisen because she knows before the story begins that her husband is having an affair with a woman, and perhaps she even senses that the woman may be Pearl Fulton.

The hysterical tone of her interior monologue is due to her attempt to compensate, to keep from acknowledging consciously what she must deeply suspect. For this reason she "hardly dared to breathe for fear of fanning . . . higher" the feeling she finds "almost unbearable." And "she hardly dared to look into the cold mirror," but when she does, she declares herself "radiant, with smiling, trembling lips, with big dark eyes, and an air of listening, waiting for something . . . divine to happen . . . that she knew must happen . . . infallibly" (338; Mansfield's ellipses). Only two words, *radiant* and *divine,* her judgments of her appearance and feeling, make affirmative a passage ironic with foreboding.

That her judgments cannot be trusted is again evident when she considers her life with Harry. First there is the significance of the arrangement of events. All is ready for the party. Waiting, Bertha looks out the windows at the pear tree "in fullest, richest bloom; it stood perfect, as though becalmed against the jade-green sky." Immediately she also sees two cats, one creeping after another. This uneasiness before animal sexuality, which becomes clear later when she identically images Eddie's departure with Miss Fulton, deepens to nervous pacing, a stifled feeling: "[A]s though overcome, she flung down on a couch and pressed her hands to her eyes. 'I'm too happy—too happy!' she murmured" (341–42). At this point she sees the "becalmed" pear tree as a symbol of her life. The distancing of whatever unbidden fears the prowling cats aroused is immediate and intense in the conscious stream which follows:

> Really—really she had everything. She was young. Harry and she were as much in love as ever, and they got on together splendidly, and were really good pals. She had an adorable baby. They didn't have to worry about money. They had this absolutely satisfactory house and garden. And friends—modern, thrilling friends, writers and painters and poets or people keen on social questions—just the kind of friends they wanted. And then there were books and there was music, and she had found a wonderful little dressmaker, and they were going abroad in the summer, and their new cook made the most superb omelettes. (342)

As the list peters out, Bertha cuts herself off quite accurately: "I'm absurd. Absurd!"

Absurd or pathetic, even her style gives her away. "Really—really—" she tries to persuade herself, assembling too many adjectives and adverbs to suggest conviction. "As much in love *as ever*" clashes ironically with "got on . . . splendidly" and "really good pals." The friends she knows too well. Her tapering off into dressmaker and cook after the diversion of the arts admits failure. For, in fact, the environment yields Bertha little satisfaction. She is cut off from both Harry and the baby. She does not "dare" question the nurse's authority; nor can she, wanting "to get in touch with [Harry] for a moment," speak to him emotionally over the phone. Even her communication with Miss Fulton is "provoking," for at a certain point Miss Fulton's frankness ceases and Bertha "couldn't yet make her out" (340–41).

That she cannot express her feelings Bertha blames on "idiotic civilization," asking "Why be given a body if you have to keep it shut up in a case like a rare, rare fiddle?" Immediately she withdraws from the image as "not quite what I mean." But feeling a similar absurdity with the nurse, she repeats it: "Why have a baby if it has to be kept—not in a case like a rare, rare fiddle—but in another woman's arms?" It is like an incremental repetition which could prove circular. The question, implicit at the end of the story, this time beginning, "Why have a husband if," may be latent in the nursery scene. For Bertha confronts not only the nurse but Pearl Fulton too, "like the poor little girl in front of the rich little girl with the doll" (338–39). This is Bertha's true image of herself; she is impoverished, denied, too absurdly civilized to act. Her frustration lies in her knowledge that, if she is in full bloom like the pear tree, she is also, like it, "becalmed."

What, then, is the reader, dependent upon Bertha's fallible point of view, to make of her relations with Harry and Pearl Fulton?[7] In a letter of 14 March 1918 Mansfield acknowledged that the newly written story was too subtle: "What I *meant* . . . was Bertha, not being an artist, was yet artist manquée enough to realise that these words and expressions were not & couldn't be hers—They were, as it were *quoted* by her, borrowed with . . . an eyebrow . . . Yet she'd none of her own. But this I agree is not permissible—I cant grant all that in my dear reader" (*Letters,* 2:121; Mansfield's ellipses). Murry had objected to the quotes. The quoted phrases are generally fashionable clichés. Bertha aspires to a more genuine mode of expression but is still inarticulate. Comparison with MP I.3, the 27 February 1918 copy sent to Murry reveals that when the story was printed, only a few of the original quotation marks had been removed. In my judgment, the careful and repeated patterning of compensatory interior monologue is belied by insistent emotional reflexes, gestures, and censored speech which reveal Bertha's unhappy awareness.

Why else has Bertha so compulsively talked to Harry of Miss Fulton, eliciting so many satisfactorily negative comments? How is it that, on his late arrival home, "she talked and laughed and positively forgot until he had come in . . . that Pearl Fulton had not turned up"? (*Positively* is the stylistic excess that arouses doubt.) Again, as they wait for Miss Fulton to come in from her taxi, why is the group uneasy in Bertha's view? "Came another tiny moment [what other moment is referred to?], while they waited, laughing and talking, just a trifle too much at their ease, a trifle too unaware. And then Miss Fulton . . . came in" (344). Of what are they "too unaware"? The implication is clearly that Bertha, suspecting some relationship between Miss Fulton and her husband, feels that the guests also know of it.

Immediately on touching the woman's arm to lead her in to dinner, Bertha starts "blazing—blazing" with what she calls "the fire of bliss." Thus she interprets the feeling she thinks she shares with her rival. Though Miss Fulton does *not* look at her, Bertha insists to herself "as if the longest, most intimate look had passed between them—as if they had said to each other: 'You, too?'—that Pearl Fulton . . . was feeling just what she was feeling" (344–45). It seems more likely that Bertha, who is acknowledgedly frigid in her sexual relations with Harry, is trying (and has been all day) to persuade herself that she feels "just what" the woman who is loved by her husband does. For Bertha knows that her evening costume of green and white echoes the pear tree, though she tells herself it is unintentional. She has also chosen the colors of the food she knows Harry desires; in her mind she quotes him on his "shameless passion for the white flesh of the lobster" and "the green of pistachio ices—green and cold like the eyelids of Egyptian dancers." But this last and most sensual of his images she cannot imitate. That is left to Miss Fulton with her "heavy eyelids" (345) and her mysterious look. She also achieves a greater appearance of coldness in her silver dress, through which she too partakes of the image of the pear tree in moonlight. The cold and silvery image implicit in the name Pearl reinforces her likeness to the moon. Beside Miss Fulton, Bertha is rather puppylike, a "pal" trying to please Harry: she could have wept like a child because he admires the soufflé.

As she stands looking at the pear tree with the other woman, Bertha makes a tremendous attempt to share Pearl Fulton's passion, simply because that is her only weapon against her rival. The pear tree, as Bertha sees it, becomes subtly phallic: "Although it was so still it seemed, like the flame of a candle, to stretch up, to point, to quiver in the bright air, to grow taller and taller as they gazed—almost to touch the rim of the round silver moon" (347).[8] But the very thought of bed, darkness, and Harry terrifies her—no matter what her dubious assertions in her panicked frame of mind. The cruelest irony she inflicts on herself is her thought that "in bed to-night" she will try to explain to Harry "[w]hat she and I have shared." That she senses they have shared Harry is clear, for all unbidden comes the emotional response to the censored thought: "At those last words something strange and almost terrifying darted into Bertha's mind." The passage which follows economically conveys both her suspicion of Harry and her fear of sexual relations, but again she censors her unconscious, imposing upon it this doubtful assertion: "For the first time in her life Bertha Young desired her husband" (348). It is, incidentally, the second and last time in the story that her artfully chosen surname is mentioned. The first time is the beginning: "Although Bertha Young was thirty. . . ." (337). The implication is obvious: Bertha is immature, and in that respect somewhat ridiculous.

But despite her flaws, Bertha has Mansfield's sympathy. Surely she was thinking of this type of woman when more than two years later she

wrote, "These half people are very queer—very tragic, really. They are
neither simple—nor are they artists. They are between the two and yet
they have the desires (no, appetites) of both" (Murry, ed. *Letters,* 577).
Though Bertha physically rejects Harry, even to seeing him grotesquely
as he surreptitiously woos Miss Fulton in the hall, she has most sensitively perceived the beauty of the pear tree. And though Bertha is
immature and has falsified herself throughout the story, she instinctively affirms life at the end. Deluded by no pathetic fallacy, she runs to the
window in her final, undeniable knowledge and sees "the pear tree was
as lovely as ever and as full of flower and as still" (350). The affirmation
retains its complexity, however, for the final emphasis is on stillness.
The pear tree continues to suggest Bertha and to be itself. If, as
Berkman well indicates, the theme of "Bliss" is "the immutability of
natural beauty in the face of human disaster (Berkman, 107), it is also
that from the human point of view such beauty offers no promise: it is
"becalmed." Fullbrook (101) sensitively comments that this ending
"leaves Bertha in absolute and bleak exclusion: the outlets for Bertha's
belated sexual flowering are suddenly blocked; a possibility is left sense-
less and dead." Even so, the"becalmed" beauty remains, perhaps like
the frozen figures on Keats's urn. Something in the complexity of this
recognition consoles, and this is the writer's way to "cry against corruption"—to challenge it.

But "Bliss" is more than a story in itself. It occupies a midposition in
a chain of stories that extends beyond "Something Childish But Very
Natural" to "Poison" in Mansfields's consideration of the failure of love
between men and women. Written immediately after "Je ne Parle pas
Français" and "Sun and Moon," "Bliss" dwells again on betrayal and,
metaphorically, on the collapse of a household no more substantial than
one molded in ice cream. This theme looks back to the earlier
"Something Childish but Very Natural," which left young Henry sitting
in a newly rented house, learning that his lover will not join him, precisely Mansfield's position in Paris when she wrote the story. The title
poem of "Something Childish," quoted again in "Poison," insists on the
intertextuality of the two stories. In "Poison" Beatrice sings, "Had I two
little feathery wings / And were a little feathery bird"—two lines,
slightly altered, of the poem. The next line, "To you I'd fly, my dear,"
had she sung it, would have made explicit the fact mentioned by
Mansfield in a letter explaining the story, that "she expects a letter from
someone calling her away (*Letters btwn.,* 325). The nameless and adoring young man recognizes the poem. "You wouldn't fly away?" he asks,

and Beatrice replies that she would fly only to meet the postman, not adding that in the expected letter lies her shifting heart.

Murry, as usual, claims to miss the point, so Mansfield herself has provided a detailed explication. Her conception of the narrator is intricate:

> The story is told by (evidently) a worldly, rather cynical (not wholly cynical) man *against* himself (but not altogether) when he was so absurdly young. You know how young by his idea of what woman is. She has been up to now, only the *vision,* only she who passes. . . . And here he has put *all* his passion into this Beatrice. . . . He of course, laughs at it now, & laughs at her. . . . But he also regrets the self who, dead privately would-have been young enough to have actually wanted to marry such a woman. . . . And the story is told by the man who gives himself away & hides his traces at the same moment. (*Letters btwn.,* 325–26)

The theme, she adds, is "the lament for youthful belief." This phrase describes "Something Childish But Very Natural" as well. In both a young man wants to marry an idolized woman, but in "Poison" the affair has progressed beyond the childish. It is, in Mansfield's words, "promiscuous love." Curiously, in "Poison," written seven years after the first one, the young man is 24, seven years older than Henry of "Something Childish." Like Edna, Beatrice smiles "dreamily," and the menace to the young man of her dreaminess is in her intensely expressed desire for mail. Even the feeling of Henry's disillusionment is reproduced through allusive similarities of image. The conclusive telegram is brought to Henry by a little girl whom he sees as a moth. As he looks at it, he thinks it perhaps make-believe, containing a make-believe snake, an idea which ironically foreshadows his poisoning. In "Poison" the postman comes as a blue beetle, and the poison itself is administered in a request for letters.

In each of the three stories something of bliss is described but in none is it real. Henry's feeling is intense but too young; it is a childish dream. For Bertha, the "bliss" is also an illusion, an effort of an older but nonetheless emotionally immature woman to attain to a feeling she does not have. The nameless narrator of "Poison" is simply deceived by his lack of experience. In "Poison," at the point of Beatrice's grossest lie— that she will not leave him—the narrator calls his condition "bliss." Ironically, trying to laugh it off, he says, "You sound as if you were saying good-bye" (567), as, of course, she is. This irony is the assertion of all Mansfield's descriptions of betrayed lovers: at the moment when they most hope they are approaching deep feelings of union, they are instead saying good-bye, discovering their immutable separateness.

In August 1920, shortly before Mansfield left for her medically pre-
scribed winter abroad, she read what she termed the "unbalanced" letters of Brett to Murry and learned with disgust that they had entered
into "more than *l'amité pure.*" "The selfishness," she raged. "Who could
count on such a man!"[9]

But awareness of the Brett affair helped Mansfield face realities in her
relationship with Murry. He had disappointed her frequently before, and
she had responded in pain. In a *Journal* (207) entry dated 12 August she
observes again his solipsism, but reaches new conclusions: "I cough and
cough. . . . And J. is silent, hangs his head, hides his face with his fingers
as though it were unendurable. 'This is what she is doing to me! Every
sound makes *my* nerves wince'. . . . If he could only for a minute . . . help
me, give *himself* up. . . . What a fate to be self-imprisoned! . . . At such
times I feel I could never get well with him. It's like having a cannonball tied to one's feet when one is trying not to drown. It is just like
that." In this realization Mansfield approaches her major turning point.
Gradually she accepts her long-resisted awareness that communication
with Murry rarely succeeds. The tone of her letters will change. He will
cease to "come walking into [her] stories" (*Letters,* 2:63). More significantly for literature, as her motivation goes beyond their unsatisfactory
relationship she is released to write the great stories.

The first letters from Menton are primarily descriptions of the beauty
of the coast and her tranquillity. She is clearly relieved to be away from
Murry, undistracted, soon able to work energetically. Hankin finds in the
letters from September through December that Mansfield is "coming to
terms . . . with her physical suffering [and] . . . spiritual isolation, in a
manner reminiscent of the great mystics." She expresses courage and
"impatience with the husband who could not fully understand the lonely path she was following" (*Letters btwn.,* 306).

In October began the spurt of creative energy: four stories—"The
Young Girl," "The Stranger," "Miss Brill," and finally "Poison," as well as
half of "The Daughters of the Late Colonel." But Mansfield also wrote
Murry of a new serenity, a remoteness, and she wrote less frequently.

On 6 October 1920 Mansfield asserts of Murry, "I do not put the slightest claim on him, nor he on me (*Letters btwn.,* 309). By 10 October he has
injudiciously sent her a letter Brett wrote to him, which makes Mansfield
"feel violently physically sick." She begs him not to let Brett touch him, but
she quickly turns to her pleasure in reading Shakespeare (*Letters btwn.,* 310).
Determinedly she defends herself from Murry's poison, but soon she will
write that story in which poison lies in a woman's expectation of a letter.

First she writes "The Stranger," an acute analysis, peculiarly sympathetic, of a man's shocked pain from jealousy. On 2 November she is in a "black mood," partly because of stormy weather, partly because she in "engulfed" in that story. She refers to her love for Murry as "my new love," a different, more distanced feeling (*Letters btwn.*, 319).

In "The Stranger" Mansfield described John Hammond's foolish lack of perception, his extreme possessiveness, and his broken, irrational sorrow. Though very different from "Poison," the two stories lead to kindred moments of truth. But the young man has cause: his woman intends to "fly away." Poor Hammond is absurdly jealous of a dead man his wife hardly knew. He wants to possess her too completely. It is more than, as Mansfield said and so many have believed, a "New Zealand story." She has enacted and thus abandoned her own possessiveness and probably realizes that Murry may stray but will not fly away. Her new knowledge will free her from the burdensome cannonball.

Undeceivably separate in the circumstances of their lives are Mansfield's *isolatoes*, Ada Moss of "Pictures," Miss Brill, Ma Parker, and that inutterably stifled Robert Salesby of "The Man Without a Temperament." But all except Robert Salesby, who is not alone, reach out for some communication, and, in different ways, all fail.

To everyone in the Pension Villa Excelsior except his wife, Salesby is a frozen Englishman. She, a sickly invalid, responds with vital interest to the lush beauty of their surroundings and to the activities of people, those in the pension and the friends who write her from abroad, but Salesby sees nothing; thrusts his mail, unread, into his pocket; admits awareness of no one's feelings except his own. In his moments of respite from caring for his wife, a duty he carries out punctiliously, aggressively, but laconically, he focuses intently upon his homesickness. He shuts out the present world in vivid recollections of the past, when his wife was well and they were in England. Deep withdrawal is evident in that he thinks of her as Jinnie in his meditations, but in the present time of the story she is unnamed. Snow and rain he recalls with pleasure. But, when from his hotel balcony he could see a sky "the colour of jade . . . many stars; an enormous white moon" and distant lightning, he stares at the balcony rail (423). Walking "past the finest villas in the town, magnificent palaces, palaces worth coming any distance to see" (419), he stares straight ahead. Twisting his ring (his symbolic fetter) as if he masochistically tormented a wound, he seems to mark time until the two years' exile for his wife's health shall be ended. And she, recognizing his state, twists his ring too.

He has come with her because she regarded him as "bread and wine," words he recalls as he remembers the doctor's unhappy verdict. But his nourishment, so fully yet so remotely administered, has rendered her apologetic, insecure, grasping at his slightest gestures to find some warmth in him. Pressed by her for an affirmation, he provides it in a typically negative word, "Rot!" (424–25) This last word of the story encompasses the corruption of their love: his view of his own position and their relationship, yet his almost submerged will to survive this damnation.

For despite the negations apparent in the views of those who do not know Salesby, and in the aridity of his actions in the present time, his interior monologues reveal a former aliveness, which indicates the author's sympathy even as she criticizes. But the final feeling is complex, for though it is not London, life is brilliantly available on this Italian Riviera: Robert need not, as his name indicates, sail by; he need not rot, but he does.[10]

The other *isolatoes* are women alone; as noted by Simone de Beauvoir, they are a recurrent Mansfield fascination. Chronologically the desperation of these women increases. In "Pictures," recast in 1919 from a 1917 version, Ada Moss seeks financial support in the despairing compromise of prostitution. In late 1920 Miss Brill is crushingly jolted, by a stranger's comment, from her comforting projections into companionship. Ma Parker's anguish must remain unexpressed for the most desolate reason: not only would her telling of the tale disturb the indifferent universe, but she can find no place even to weep.

Ranging from second-rate artist through impoverished gentlewoman to lowly, uneducated old cleaning woman, these stories increase in painful effect. Ada Moss, though down-and-out, remains jaunty and continues to act, even if in her own defeat. Physically she is somewhat comic. Miss Brill, however, despite her inaccuracies, engages the reader's affection for her bright, sensitive enjoyment of the world she fabricates in the Jardins Publiques. When her "hierarchy of unrealities"[11] is shattered, her only diversion from dull weekday work and her pleasure in her shabby furpiece—in sum, her joy—have been taken away. The catastrophic descent from illusory pleasure is intensified by being revealed from her viewpoint. No distancing of emotion is allowed as the reader follows her train of thought and feeling. She has smiled, albeit tearfully and sentimentally, at the notion of a communion in song in the park. Stalwartly she has not merely stared like those "funny" ones she has noticed: "They were odd, silent, nearly all old, and from the way they stared they looked as though they'd just come from dark little rooms or even—cupboards!" The reader but not Miss Brill sees the similarity to her furpiece. But after the callous boy, "the hero," reiteratively dwells on "that stupid old thing" and "her silly old mug" she creeps off home and conclusively recognizes her true kinship: "She . . . went into the little dark room—her room like a cupboard." When she packs away the furpiece and "thought she heard something crying" (551–54), her identification with that object is so complete that the reader fears she weeps and yet is too valiant to acknowledge it. Painfully, the reader also fears that perhaps for the last time she has "rubbed the life back into the dim little eyes" (549).

Expressing her affection for Miss Brill, Mansfield told Murry, "One writes (*one* reason why is) because one does care so passionately that one *must* show it—one must declare one's love" (Murry, ed. *Letters*, 598). That it was her mode of expressing faith is evident in her description of the mood in which she composed the story: "Last night I walked about and saw the new moon with the old moon in her arms and the lights in the water and the hollow pools full of stars—and lamented there was no God. But I came in and wrote *Miss Brill* instead; which is my insect Magnificat now and always" (*Letters btwn.*, 321). In her perpetuation of awareness of Miss Brill's inmost nature, Mansfield herself makes the statement of the becalmed pear tree outside Bertha Young's window.

In September 1921 Mansfield copied into a notebook the final passages of Chekhov's story "Misery" and added, "I would see every single French short story up the chimney for this. It's one of the masterpieces of the world" (*Journal*, 263). She had written one of very similar approach in "The Life of Ma Parker." It, with "The Lady's Maid," provides two studies of isolation in servants. "The Lady's Maid" poured out the story of her life, shriveled by the will of her mistress, in a monologue which implied the presence of a kind guest who listened long past bedtime. Ma Parker met only embarrassed indifference in the literary gentleman she served. In this Mansfield goes Chekhov one better. His bereft Iona seeks sympathy for the death of his son first from his cab fares, a military officer, and three abusive, bad-tempered young men; then from a doorman; and finally from a fellow cabman who falls asleep. "Ordinary" people are conventionally expected to make ordinary, insensitive responses. But Ma Parker's literary gentleman, who by his very trade should be empathetic, is only patronizing and later parsimonious, as he badgers his hired "hag" about a teaspoon of cocoa. Ma Parker must review her life story to herself. Disaster after disaster goes through her mind as she cleans the flat. No one has ever seen her break down, but now, with the death of her grandson, she can bear no more, she wants to cry: "If she could only cry now, cry for a long time, over everything, beginning with her first place and the cruel cook, going on to the doctor's, and then the seven little ones, death of her husband, the children's leaving her, and all the years of misery that led up to Lennie." (490).

Again her situation is worse than the one Chekhov portrayed. Iona at last seeks out his horse and tells the whole story. But for Ma Parker in her extremity there is not even a place for weeping. The gentleman's flat is out of the question. At home she would frighten her daughter. In public she would be reprimanded by a policeman. Her plight is not only isolation but utter inability to relieve her pain by any means.

From September into December 1920 Mansfield steadfastly continued to write, while she gradually acknowledged and finally accepted her need to withdraw from expectations of Murry. In pain she worked her way toward a distanced relationship.

The climactic blowup approached in mid-November, when Murry gave *Sphere,* for advertising use, an old Mansfield photograph which she had never liked. She took his acceptance of—perhaps his preference for—the earlier image as evidence that he no longer knew her. "I am not that woman," she wrote angrily. "I have been ill for nearly four years—and I am changed changed—not the same." The next day she sent Murry a "business letter," asking him to put her writing and publicity into the hands of an agent (*Letters btwn.,* 322–23). Of course, telegrams and letters followed, intended to soften the blow. But she got the new agent almost immediately. Murry's replies are apparently not extant, but one intuits his obtuse responses to Mansfield's writing when she defends the punctuation of "The Stranger" and explicates "Poison" (*Letters btwn.,* 324–25).

On 8 December she resigns from reviewing books for the *Athenaeum,* explaining that the strain is affecting her health. She also rebukes Murry for not sending her their Corona typewriter, which would have saved her from burdensome writing by hand (*Letters btwn.,* 329–30). But she was struggling for a tranquil reconciliation, asking him to "help me keep all fair—all fine and serene" (*Letters btwn.,* 334). Tactlessly Murry sent her a maudlin, confessional letter, relating a sequence of repressed amorous beginnings with, sequentially, Anne Drey, Mrs. Bonamy Dobrey, a Leicester Square "tart," Dorothy Brett, and his new friend the Princess Bibesco. Mansfield wired, "STOP TORMENTING ME WITH THESE FALSE DEPRESSING LETTERS . . . BE A MAN OR DONT WRITE ME" (*Letters btwn.,* 332–34).

In a letter the same day Mansfield explains that her previous "writing self . . . was merged in my personal self. I felt conscious of you—to the exclusion of almost everything. . . . But now I do not." To mollify she adds, "You are dearer than anyone in the world to me—but more than anything else . . . I want to write." A wire recants two days later (*Letters btwn.*, 334–35). But the seesaw of letters throughout 1920 shows Mansfield steadily persuading herself of Murry's inadequacy. Confronting and accepting her loss of the imagined Murry has led her to her final theme, the failure of love between human beings, the swift passing of beauty, and the indifference which prevents communication—these became the painful themes of Mansfield's maturity.

"Poison" may be her last message to Murry; "The Stranger," her last apology. In late December 1920 she set down her credo:

> I should like this to be accepted as my confession.
> There is no limit to human suffering. When one thinks: " . . . —now I can go no deeper," one goes deeper. And so it is forever. . . . Suffering is boundless, it is eternity.
> . . . .
> Everything in life that we really accept undergoes a change. So suffering must become Love. . . . . . I must pass from personal love . . . to greater love. I must give to the whole of life what I gave to him.
> . . . .
> I must turn *to work*. I must put my agony into something, change it. "Sorrow shall be changed into joy" (*Journal*, 228–29).

A few days after Murry reached Menton for Christmas holidays, Mansfield confirmed her new attitude: "I thought of Jack . . . within reach . . . . I remembered there was a time when this thought was a distraction . . . . It took away my power to work . . . . I . . . made him my short story. But that belongs to the Past" (*Journal*, 233).

The turn did not come immediately. She had yet to write, early in 1921, "The Life of Ma Parker." Then, though Murry quit the *Athenaeum* and joined her in Menton at the end of February, she lay dormant, ill and exhausted for several months. But in July the creative spurt began, and she wrote eleven stories by the end of January. She tapped now the vein of her truest love: seven of the stories were laid in New Zealand. With several of them she was very much dissatisfied. But in the brief time of September and October she wrote three memorable stories, "At the Bay," "The Garden Party," and "The Doll's House." These stories pursue the consideration of order begun in "Prelude"; however, the writer is determined upon acceptance. Nothing of the caustic Mansfield remains. Death has become part of order, and ugliness is no longer overwhelming. The dominant tone and organization of attitudes suggest an affirmation.

In "At the Bay" are many passages which dwell with fondness on the quality of the living. Stanley, despite all his foibles—his little selfishnesses, his materialism, his lack of imagination—is a man to love, and the cool Linda, who still rejects her children, fears childbearing, and remains aloof from most of life, does love Stanley. She herself has become a more sympathetic character, and life exudes its radiance in the grandmother, in Mrs. Stubbs, and especially in the children.

The debate between order and disorder is first engaged in by Stanley and Jonathan as they bathe in the sea. Stanley is going to work and has "no time to—to—to fool about." Jonathan speculates on his tension and makes his own avowal: "There was something pathetic in [Stanley's] determination to make a job of everything. . . . That was the way to live [like the sea]—carelessly, recklessly, spending oneself. . . . To take things easy, not to fight against the ebb and flow of life, but to give way to it— that was what was needed. It was this tension that was all wrong. To live—to live" (267). But once out of the sea, because he has stayed in too long, Jonathan is cold and tense himself, "as though some one was wringing the blood out of him" (268). With ironic immediacy he has yielded in this change of mood to the ebb and flow.

Later he expresses to Linda his hatred for his routine job: "I'm like an insect that's flown into a room of its own accord. I dash against the walls, dash against the windows, flop against the ceiling, do everything on God's earth, in fact, except fly out again. And all the while I'm thinking . . . 'The shortness of life! The shortness of life!' " But he cannot escape from the order against which he rebels so violently. Why? Because "it's not allowed, it's forbidden, it's against the insect law, to stop banging and flopping and crawling up the pane even for an instant." Then "in a changed voice, as if he were confiding a secret," he tells Linda the real reason: "Weak. . . . No stamina. No anchor. No guiding principle" (292–93). Paradoxically, he cannot challenge order because nothing holds him fast in the ebb and flow; he has no order in himself. Yet in this story dominated by the image of the sea, there is a continual changing of positions among the characters. Jonathan too can stand for order. When he seeks his children in the evening, he is for a moment a frightening face looking out of the dark through the washhouse window. The orderly game becomes a chaos of fear. But then the door opens and he is revealed, Uncle Jonathan, the comforting representative of adult order.

In Stanley's tensions the same paradox emerges. Exceedingly neat and conscious of time, he appears at the breakfast table. The chaotic 25 minutes until the coach arrives are spent demanding services to which he is clearly accustomed. Order for Stanley means disorder for the household. Even Alice, the servant girl, is pulled into the hunt for his walking stick. All the women are thankful when he is gone. Linda compares the experience to "living in a house that couldn't be cured of the habit of catching on fire, on a ship that got wrecked every day" (279).

Apparently too, Stanley's behavior ebbs and flows, for Linda also knows "a timid, sensitive, innocent Stanley who knelt down every night to say his prayers, and who longed to be good." This is a loyal, honest, simple man, who suffers at any deceit from those he believes in. Then, like Jonathan, Stanley is imaged as a "trapped beast," wildness growing distraught at a violation of his order. For his is a wrong kind of order, order involving tension. But Jonathan, because of his conflict with the "masculine role" Stanley exemplifies, is also doomed to continual tension. The kinship yet contrast of the two men displays a fluidity of gender roles in both. Kaplan rightly describes the participation of Linda and Beryl in this theme.[12]

The children play at being beasts, kept in order by the rules of the game as laid down by Pip. Secure in this pattern, they have escaped the excessive order of the Samuel Joseph children, for whose undisciplined natures an "awful" daily program is planned and administered by their lady-help, complete with police whistle. Only feminist Kezia runs counter to Pip's male conventions. Despite protests, she is a bee, an insect (like Jonathan) rather than an animal. And to help Lottie, who is too young to play well, she delays the game, playing without competitive spirit. Kezia's sympathies are such that she challenges order for the sake of joy.

In a scene of philosophical content, near in time to the story's high noon, Kezia, learning from her grandmother that it is in the order of events that they should both someday die, protests: *"You're* not to die." Kezia was very decided (283). But the seriousness and anxiety ebb to a tickling match.

Again, in Kezia's case order and disorder are sometimes one. Beryl scolds her for messy eating, and sister Isabel agrees. But Kezia feels that "she had only dug a river down the middle of her porridge, filled it, and was eating the banks away." (269). To her it is an order and she controls its destruction. Kezia's self-esteem builds for her a tensionless order.

A comical merging of order and disorder occurs at Mrs. Stubbs's shop: "On the veranda there hung a long string of bathing dresses, clinging together as though they'd just been rescued from the sea . . . and beside them there hung a cluster of sand-shoes so extraordinarily mixed that to get at one pair you had to tear apart and forcibly separate at least fifty" (285). Mrs. Stubbs, looking "like a friendly brigand," welcomes the restrained and proper Alice "so warmly that she found it quite difficult to keep up her 'manners.' They consisted of persistent little coughs and hems, pulls at her gloves, tweaks at her skirt, and a curious difficulty in seeing what was set before her or understanding what was said." As they shout to be heard above a roaring Primus, the display of Mrs. Stubbs's new photographs is broad, chaotic comedy:

> Mrs. Stubbs sat in an arm-chair, leaning very much to one side. There was a look of mild astonishment on her large face, and well there might be. For though the arm-chair stood on a carpet, to the left of it, miraculously skirting the carpet-border, there was a dashing waterfall. On her right stood a Grecian pillar with a giant fern-tree on either side of it, and in the background towered a gaunt mountain, pale with snow.
> "It's a nice style, isn't it?" shouted Mrs. Stubbs. (286)

To end the scene, echoing Linda's view of marriage, she advises Alice that "Freedom's best," and Alice, with typical rigidity, recoils: "Freedom! Alice gave a loud, silly little titter. She felt awkward. Her mind flew back to her own kitching. Ever so queer! She wanted to be back in it again" (287).

At the approximate center of the story, near the noon of its single day in which time is so carefully noted from before dawn into darkness,[13] Linda explores the mystery that is life and emerges with a more affirmative view than that found in "Prelude." Her focal position at the high point of story time in "At the Bay" indicates the importance of her conclusions, and she will in the end receive some implicit confirmation from the all-enveloping sea.

Examining the beauty of the flowers and musing on their swift mutability, Linda asks the crucial question: "Why, then, flower at all? Who takes the trouble—or the joy—to make all these things that are wasted, wasted. . . . It was uncanny" (278; Mansfield's ellipsis). She does not recognize it yet, but the immediate answer, her baby boy, lies beside her on the grass, his head turned away, asleep. That her question involves, more seriously than for Kezia, the fear of her own death appears in her next consideration of the flowers: "If only one had time to look at these flowers long enough, time to get over the sense of novelty and strangeness, time to know them! But as soon as one paused to part the petals, to discover the underside of the leaf, along came Life and one was swept away. . . . Along came Life like a wind and she was seized and shaken; she had to go. . . . Was there no escape?" (278). Her life appears to be spent in calming the excited Stanley Burnell and fearing childbirth, the latter made worse because "she did not love her children."

But as this thought runs through her mind, she discovers that the boy is awake. He smiles, and Linda finds her answer:

> There was something so quaint, so unexpected about that smile that Linda smiled herself. But she checked herself and said to the boy coldly, "I don't like babies."
> "Don't like babies?" The boy couldn't believe her. "Don't like me?" He waved his arms foolishly at his mother.
> . . . .
> Linda was so astonished at the confidence of this little creature. . . .
> Ah no, be sincere. That was not what she felt; it was something far different, it was something so new, so. . . . The tears danced in her eyes; she breathed in a small whisper to the boy, "Hallo, my funny!" (280; Mansfield's ellipses).

Out of the order of things which brings forth children in pain and fades the flowers too soon Linda finds at last that her reward is the brief beauty of love. Her acceptance has not lessened when later in the evening she listens to Jonathan's unhappy and futile rebellion. Observing the beauty of evening, she or the author (it is not clear here which) recognizes that a cruel meaning may linger in sunset: "Sometimes when those beams of light show in the sky they are very awful. They remind you that up there sits Jehovah, the jealous God, the Almighty, Whose eye is upon you. . . . You remember that at His coming the whole world will shake into one ruined graveyard; the cold, bright angels will drive you this way and that, and there will be no time to explain what could be explained so simply" (293–94).

Linda's final thought, however, is different: "But to-night it seemed to Linda there was something infinitely joyful and loving in those silver beams. And now no sound came from the sea. It breathed softly as if it would draw the tender, joyful beauty into its own bosom." The ebb and flow continues as Jonathan interrupts with, "It's all wrong, it's all wrong," but his voice is shadowy (294). For Linda, the question is answered.

Mansfield, agreeing with Chekhov that a writer poses questions but does not answer them, devotes the last incident to Beryl's exploration. All day Beryl has experimented with disorder and ugliness, but she herself appears to prefer order and is repelled by the evil she encounters. Her experience at the beach with Mrs. Harry Kemper parallels that in the evening with Mr. Harry Kemper. These two are so alike that, when the women are swimming, Beryl sees with dismay that the unattractive, disorderly creature looks "like a horrible caricature of her husband" (277). The ebb-and-flow mingling of freedom and repression characterizes both incidents. The tense, "burnt out" Mrs. Kemper flouts the conventions of the summer resort and urges the inhibited Beryl to freedom: "I believe in pretty girls having a good time. . . . Enjoy yourself" (277). But as they undress for swimming, it is Mrs. Kemper, not Beryl, who is seen to have bound her body in corset stays.

That Beryl's chance to "enjoy herself" should be offered by Mr. Kemper is an apt irony. As the adventure begins, Beryl, in a romantic reverie in her room, feels the disorder of darkness. She is a "conspirator" before she sees a strange man, perhaps a burglar, in the garden. Having recognized him, she refuses his invitation on conventional, orderly grounds, but his challenge lures her outside. When he forcibly embraces her, constraining her to a freedom, she, repelling it, "wrenched free."

The sea serves many purposes throughout the story. It is the scene of Stanley's conflict with Jonathan, Beryl's adventure with Mrs. Kemper, and the children's morning play. Though it creates natural beauty, the final experiences of all whose feelings are described in contact with the sea are unpleasant. Rewarded at first, Stanley and Jonathan leave it tense. Beryl, aware of the warm blue, silver, and golden beauty, sees Mrs. Kemper as a rat in the sea and feels the woman's poison enter her there. Even little Lottie, "when a bigger wave than usual, an old whiskery one, came lolloping along in her direction, . . . scrambled to her feet with a face of horror and flew up the beach again" (274). Around high noon, just after Linda has attained acceptance of the order of life and death and just before Kezia will challenge death with laughter, the beach is deserted, but under the fiery sun the sea reveals a reflected but mysterious world. It is as though the sea, which Linda, who attains the only insight of the story, never goes near, would maintain somehow, in its ebb and flow, its secret and its tension. The order of the sea reflects rocks as beasts and the world upside down—a disorder.

Final comment, then, is left to the sea. The isolated emphasis that is the single, short paragraph of section 13 implies that it pictures the alternate rise and fall of emotion, negation and affirmation of attitude throughout the story: "A cloud, small, serene, floated across the moon. In that moment of darkness the sea sounded deep, troubled. Then the cloud sailed away, and the sound of the sea was a vague murmur, as though it waked out of a dark dream. All was still" (299).

The sea has dominated the entire story. In the opening all the land is enveloped, hidden by "sea-mist." The first section is like the overture to a piece of pastoral music, as a shepherd, his dog, and a flock of sheep appear out of the mist. The shepherd whistles, smokes a pipe, then whistles again as he disappears. The sheep bleat and are answered by ghostly herds under the sea. Florrie, the Burnell's cat and the only member of the resort colony to see this passage, arches her back at the dog, who sensibly (for a dog) ignores her. None of these characters appear again except Florrie, but they have suggested, as the opening bars should, the basic themes of the composition. The dog and the shepherd are responsible order among the feckless sheep, and they are very much at ease, very relaxed in the world in which they perform their task. They are order without tension, the ideal natural order, probably the order of acceptance and love which Linda discovers. But the independent cat rejects the ordering dog.

Florrie's reappearance in section 11 acts as a musical motif to recall the images and feeling of the opening, to effect a return of the mind to that tranquillity just as Stanley, much subdued but still expressing his tensions, returns. The Stanley and Linda theme is resolved peacefully; there is the excited flurry of Beryl's section; and then the coda, back where Florrie has pointed the way, with the sea and the closing direction.

Far less complicated in structure and, perhaps for that reason, more immediately moving are the acceptances of "The Garden-Party" and "The Doll's House." In "The Garden-Party" Laura's struggle against convention and her uneasy search for her role are made clear by her disposal of the bread and butter she takes to the lawn at the beginning of the day. She carries it out in a moment of reckless joy at the beauty, excitement, and promise of the day. She hides it from the workmen, fearing to be thought childish. Then, as her fellow-feeling grows, she eats it in big bites, imagining herself like "a work–girl" (536).

She is trying to discover right behavior, and she suspects uneasily that it is not to be found in what is conventionally correct. She does not feel, before the haggard look of a pale workman, that it is right to have a band for their party. Her suggestions for the location of the marquee are wrong, but the right place conceals the lovely karaka-trees. Her more intense notion that the party should be stopped because a man has been killed is called absurd and extravagant by the practical sister Jose, and it first amuses and then annoys her mother. Later she is sure that to take the remains of the party food to the bereaved family is wrong, and again she is overruled. "Run down just as you are," bids her mother, airily unaware of the feelings of the poor, and Laura goes, awkwardly embarrassed by the mission, by her party dress, and by her hat (546).

It is the hat which distracted her from her protest against the party,[14] just as Pat's earrings distracted a younger Kezia from a protest against death in "Prelude." So it is appropriate that before the dead young man, to whom she must say something, Laura says, "Forgive my hat" (548).

This incongruous, even comic remark at the moment of Laura's greatest seriousness and greatest childishness ("she gave a loud childish sob") renders her viewing of the body convincing and her ambivalent response likely. From the fair copy, dated 14 October 1920 and sent to Murry, Mansfield has deleted passages that conflict with Laura's unexpected elation. A few false starts remain in the following passages, later crossed out:

> Laura was so shocked. She had never seen a dead body before. She'd never [illegible] and like she reached. At her side Em's sister gave a curious hissing sound as though she was satisfied
>
> . . . .
>   To the astonishment of Em's sister Laura suddenly put her hand over her face. (MP, Box 1, 18)

In the final version the distraction of Em's sister is eliminated, and the reader is left to intuit the unspeakable in Laura's inarticulate response. Seeing the young man as "wonderful, beautiful . . . this marvel," she tries to communicate the experience to her brother. As death and the party have existed side by side, so do her exaltation and her tears. Again the menace has merged with and become beauty (548–49).

As she continued to come to terms with the alternation of pain and joy, of hope and desolation—as she faced the imminent likelihood of her death—in a letter of 13 March 1922 Mansfield commented on the insight which Laura struggles to make articulate: "The diversity of life and how we try to fit in everything, Death included. That is bewildering for a person of Laura's age. She feels things ought to happen differently. . . . But life isn't like that. We haven't the ordering of it. Laura says, 'But

all these things must not happen at once.' And Life answers, "Why not?
. . . " And they *do* all happen, it is inevitable. And it seems to me there is
beauty in that inevitability" (Murry, ed., *Letters,* 2:454).

"The Doll's House" is Mansfield's last portrait of Kezia, who, as
always, in her misbehavior does the right thing. The rhythms of the
story oscillate between pleasure and pain: joy at the minute perfection of
the doll's house, snobbery among adults and imitative little girls, which
accelerates twice to psychic assault on the socially outcast, scapegoated
Kelvey children. Disobedient Kezia offers momentary relief when she
grants a brief vision of the house to the cruelly despised and derided
Kelveys. Their appreciation is interrupted by Beryl's angry, abusive
words, and pain again pervades the story. The final emotional turn in the
words of "our Els" does not exclude that pain but conveys what
Mansfield was learning in the last years of her life.

When Kezia had announced in the schoolyard that the little lamp
was best of all, "nobody paid any attention." But though she had no
time to point it out to the Kelveys, after they have fled, Else, whom
"nobody had ever seen . . . smile" and who rarely spoke, does smile and
speak. In her soft words, "I seen the little lamp" (577), is affirmation rising from the simplest, most helplessly wretched level that Katherine
Mansfield will describe. The writer has come far from the little boy's
wailing in "Sun and Moon" at the melted, broken ice cream house. By a
strenuous effort of will and imagination, she defied for a time all of the
negative pressures laid upon her by ill health and by personal failures in
her relationship with Murry. In the years of strain leading, she suspected,
to her dying, she hopefully proclaimed that there was beauty in any ugliness—even in death.

On page 10 of the Newberry manuscript of "The Doll's House" (MP,
Box 1, 11), opposite the end of the story, Mansfield has drawn three elephant heads. Was she thinking in this final house story of "The
Elephant," the Hampstead house she and Murry bought in August
1920, where she had tried to create a home? Ill health drove her away.
She was able to live there less than a year and a half. In March 1921 they
had given it up, and she wrote to LM, who was clearing out the house,
"I wish I was back in that Hampstead house—wafted to the top stairs to
look out the windows to see if the lemon verbena is still alive. It should
have been a perfect little house. It never came to flower."[15]

The feeling, as in "The Doll's House," is mixed. She regretted the
loss, but she held on to the beauty.

Chapter Six

"Will There Be a Ripple . . . ?"

It remains to describe the final artistry of Katherine Mansfield in terms of three stories which display her technique brought to a fine finish and her attitudes expressed at their greatest depth. In the late months of 1920, while exploring the theme of isolation, she wrote "The Stranger" and "The Daughters of the Late Colonel." "The Fly," her next-to-last completed story, was composed in February 22, while she underwent drastic treatment for tuberculosis.

These three episodes of discovery embody the typical Mansfield work. The subject in each is people who suffer some emotional loss. In each instance the characters are affected by a physical death, but it becomes clear that this death is not central in the author's mind; she delineates, instead, spiritual death in her main characters, death of which none of them is completely aware. All of these stories are, in Mansfield's phrase, "a cry against corruption"—specifically against failure of the spirit.

The action is typically slight: a man visits with a friend, then kills a fly; a man meets his wife's ship, takes her to a hotel, and is disheartened by her account of a shipboard experience; two women try vaguely to organize their affairs after the death of their father. The most complicated structure, that of "The Daughters of the Late Colonel," surrounds the least action. The other two are brief incidents, largely chronological in order, though in "The Stranger" Janey tells briefly of the death of the young man and in "The Fly" Woodifield remembers his daughters' trip to Belgium and the boss recalls briefly his son's participation in the business. Both these stories open on highly particularized scenes and are immediately focused in the consciousness of the protagonist, after which the narrator has little access to any other awareness. "The Daughters of the Late Colonel" is a virtuoso piece in the use of multipersonal viewpoint.

Since the tone of the narrator is that of the interior monologues, it is difficult to locate a purely narrative segment in any of the stories. The treatment is dramatic, with summary and generalization avoided by the author. The reader must infer from the gestures and the speech of the characters what their natures are and what Mansfield means to convey.

She builds her stories toward such moments of discovery. John Hammond states and the colonel's daughters intimate what they have realized, but the boss can reach no conclusion. In each case, the implicit revelation is greater for the reader than for the characters. The dramatic effect is increased by this irony of a more accurate knowledge in the audience, a knowledge, however, which the author does not define. This approach represents the mature Mansfield, practicing her ideal of objective narrative, devoid of the author's intrusive voice.

"The Stranger" describes the death of the heart of John Hammond, who discovers that, as he has feared, his wife is not wholly his own. She extends a tenderness that he feels is denied him, not only to their children, whom he rivals, but to a dying stranger. The reader discovers that they too are strangers: Hammond, who wants too much of a wife, and Janey, who does not completely understand—or more likely, chooses to avoid—his will to possess her utterly.

The two men involved in this story are parallel in that one apparently died of feelings similar to the other's, agitation at the homecoming. The young stranger died of a weak heart. Janey explains, "He had a severe attack in the afternoon—excitement—nervousness, I think, about arriving. And after that he never recovered" (457). In the first segment of the story Hammond wins the reader's sympathy by his excitement as he paces the wharf, waiting for his wife's ship to dock. His warmth toward the others waiting is egocentrically caused by his assumption that Janey's arrival somehow means something to them too. He tries to divert a child from her hunger for tea, paces, chats affably, and finally gives away all his cigars because he sees his wife on the approaching ship. As the ship turns, he cannot tell "whether that deep throbbing was her engines or his heart . . . He had to nerve himself to bear it, whatever it was" (448). The end of the story implies that Hammond, like the other stranger, never recovered.

But Hammond's metaphorical death results from his intensely possessive feeling; he wants more than can be demanded of an individual. There are many evidences that he knows this. When he embraces Janey in her cabin, "again, as always, he had the feeling he was holding something that never was quite his—his" (453). In the hotel he says, "I feel I'll never have you to myself again" (454), and this is his conclusion upon her revelation of the stranger's death in her arms. Even with her at last in his arms, his interior monologue, which recounts most of the story, reveals his insecurity: "But just as when he embraced her he felt she would fly away, so Hammond never knew—never knew for dead certain

that she was as glad as he was. . . . Would he always have this craving—
this pang like hunger, somehow, to make Janey so much part of him that
there wasn't any of her to escape? He wanted to blot out everybody,
everything" (455). His feelings are rendered as understandably pathetic,
but they lead him to self-exile.

The reader is soon certain that Janey is not so glad as her husband at
their meeting, for they are, from the beginning, at cross-purposes.
Seeing her from afar, Hammond must turn to his cigar case to compose
himself, but when he looks again, she is "watching him, ready for him."
At his warm greeting, she meets him with a "cool little voice" and a
"half-smile." He brushes aside her concern for the children, and he has
left at the hotel their letters, which she would like immediately. Later, in
the hotel, he selfishly fails to understand that she would like to read
these letters, and he even resents them, "tucked into her frilled blouse"
and rustling there when he has her on his knee.[1] He is in a rush to get
her away from the ship, but she must make her polite farewells to fellow
passengers, the captain, and the doctor. His feeling that "he'd got her" is
belied when, in the cab, after a bit she "gently drew her hand away."
Even by the removal of her hat she delays coming to sit on Hammond's
lap, and though then she lies on his breast, he feels her so remote that he
must demand, "Kiss me, Janey! You kiss me." But this too is not adequate. To him it seems that her kiss "confirmed what they were saying,
signed the contract. But that wasn't what he wanted; that wasn't at all
what he thirsted for" (449–56).

When they entered the hotel room, the fire Hammond had ordered
was blazing, as was his passion. As Janey begins to explain the delay in
docking, she and Hammond watch the fire die. The sequence of fire
images accompanies his emotional death and echoes a tonal foreshadowing against which he had protested on the dock. He noted then the coming darkness and waved his umbrella as though to keep it off. "But the
dusk came slowly, spreading like a slow stain over the water." In their
room "[t]he flames hurried—hurried over the coals, flickered, fell" (447,
456). Janey tells her story of the death of the young man.

When she reveals, "He died in my arms," the effect on Hammond is
like that of the stranger's heart attack: "The blow was so sudden that
Hammond thought he would faint. He couldn't move; he couldn't
breathe. He felt all his strength flowing—flowing into the big dark
chair." Unaware, Janey continues, and his response intensifies: "Ah, my
God, what was she saying! What was she doing to him! This would kill

him!" (456). Snow images, mingled with the dying fire, symbolize his feelings. As Janey ends her story and is silent,

> her words, so light, so soft, so chill, seemed to hover in the air, to rain into his breast like snow.
> The fire had gone red. Now it fell with a sharp sound and the room was colder. Cold crept up his arms. The room was huge, immense, glittering. It filled his whole world. There was the great blind bed, with his coat flung across it like some headless man saying his prayers (457).

Here, in full stride, Katherine Mansfield carries the technique of poetry into the short story. The rhythms of image and sound orchestrate the empty, frozen, disintegrated quality of Hammond's realization.

But Janey, a stranger to her stranger, cannot or will not understand his attitude. She wonders at him. At his moan " . . . [W]hy *you?*" she "turned quickly, quickly searched his face. 'You don't *mind,* John, do you?' she asked. 'You don't—It's nothing to do with you and me.' " But she senses his drop in mood and asks again, "You're not—sorry I told you, John darling? It hasn't made you sad? It hasn't spoilt our evening—our being alone together?" (457).

When Janey first told him that a young man had died at sea, Hammond was uneasy: "It was in some queer way, as though he and Janey had met a funeral on their way to the hotel" (456). Now he receives her account as if it were his own funeral. At her doubtful question, in his mind the tragedy is completed. He tells himself: "They would never be alone together again" (458). He is crushed, paradoxically, by his recognition of what he has always suspected: he cannot, no matter how well he plans the occasion, ever have total possession of Janey. Whether he is right or wrong in his appraisal, he cannot communicate his pain to her. Thus they remain strangers, neither understanding the other. The antithetic "alone together" describes their permanent situation, past and present.

Mansfield sympathized completely with her characters, but she did not consider their plight tragic. While composing, she reported to Murry that she was in a "black mood": "*I am writing. . . .* [A]nd until this story is finished I am engulfed. It's not a tragic story either." But it possessed her: "I've *been* this man, *been* this woman. . . . I've been a seagull hovering at the stern and a hotel porter whistling through his teeth. . . . [O]ne IS the spectacle for the time" (*Letters btwn.,* 319,321).

Despite her avowed empathy, she limits herself as an author. Opening the story as the omniscient author, she shifts the viewpoint into the consciousness of John Hammond with the words "But what a fool" (446). From that moment on, the author may reveal a little more of Hammond's consciousness than he himself recognizes, but largely the story is seen through his eyes. The ironic truth of his first words about himself indicates the author's view of his character: his misery is of his own making because of his lack of understanding, his inability to share. In the opening scene he is only lamenting his lack of field glasses and his resulting inability to see Janey on the ship, but his failure is a greater one: he cannot *see* Janey, no matter how close he gets. When, in his arms, she tells of the stranger who died in hers, his response reveals to the reader that they are also strangers and yet that it need not be. In this John Hammond is, as he said, a fool, a pathetically mistaken man.[2]

"The Daughters of the Late Colonel" are pathetically wasted women, but Mansfield has described their condition, because it is absurd, in a series of loving yet comic scenes. Josephine and Constantia, two middle-aged women[3] who have spent their lives taking care of an irascible father and keeping out of his way, have been so intimidated by the experience that after his death they are unable to cope with his nurse and the maid. Their timidity extends to being unable to believe that the colonel is really dead. As a result, their tentative efforts to make decisions or to take practical action are often hilarious.

Many jokes rise from the funeral situation. Constantia, always ready with an inappropriate word, hopes for "a good one that will last." Josephine panics at the cemetery because they have buried Father without his permission and she is certain that "he was bound to find out sooner or later." She even imagines him complaining about the bills. Constantia reassures her: "We couldn't have kept him, Jug—we couldn't have kept him unburied. At any rate, not in a flat that size." But fantastically Josephine feels that they "ought to have tried to, just for a time at least," and she is sure that he will never forgive them (470). Equally absurd is their fear of disturbing his room, which becomes a conviction that he is in the chest of drawers "ready to spring." Constantia triumphs on this occasion. "Why shouldn't we be weak for once in our lives, Jug?" she says, and boldly locks the wardrobe (472). To point up the paradox, Josephine recalls Constantia's last bold act, in long-ago childhood, when she had pushed their brother Benny into a pond.

An extended memory of a scene at tea with their nephew Cyril, which culminates in a ridiculous attempt to make the deaf colonel hear that

Cyril's father still likes meringues, characterizes these women as inept but hopeful in dealing with their bullying father. Their efforts to please Cyril are, of course, rendered more pathetic by his youthful, rushed lack of appreciation.

Eleven sections of the story characterize them as amusingly fearful, mild, kind women. In the twelfth, at the sound of a barrel-organ, they jump, still under their father's spell, to send the organ-grinder away, and suddenly realization comes: they need never stop him again; they will never again hear their father pounding his stick and giving angry orders. They smile strangely and hear the barrel-organ play, *"It will never thump again. . . . A week since father died"* (481). Supported by images of music and increasing sunlight, they ponder and for a moment reach out toward some future change in their situation. But it is a sunlight which "thieved its way in," a "thieving sun" which cannot free them. Each starts to speak her thoughts; thus by their interruptions they stop one another. Neither will continue, but the scene with the wardrobe, where Constantia knew what was in her sister's mind, implies that she knows here as well. "Don't be absurd, Con," (483) says Josephine, and each implores the other to speak.

But they *are* absurd. Each longed for sexual fulfillment. Vague Constantia expressed her desire by symbolic gestures: standing before the Buddha in the drawing room, she remembers the nights she had lain there in her nightgown, as if "crucified" before the moon, and recalls making up songs, alone beside the "restless" sea. Only then did "she really [feel] herself" (482–83). Pragmatic Josephine forgets to be practical. She watches the sun creep across to her mother's photograph and wonders whether, if their mother hadn't died, she and Constantia might have married. In her memory of the lack of men and of the single absurd opportunity, she reverts to practicality.

These women are like the sparrows Josephine heard, whose "queer little crying noise" (482) she knew was inside her. They are like the mouse Constantia felt so sorry for that she couldn't "think how they manage to live at all" (465). These animal images in the beginning and end of the story unify it and spell out their doom, as the sun is symbolically replaced by a cloud. Both assert they have forgotten what they wished to say, but this is credible only in the case of the vague Constantia. With Josephine it seems a practical denial.

Mansfield was disappointed that very few understood the story. Explaining to William Gerhardi, she wrote that though at first she saw the two sisters as amusing, when she looked deeper, she "bowed down to the beauty that was in their lives." All, she continued, led "up to that last paragraph, when my two flowerless ones turned with that timid gesture. . . . And after that . . . they died as surely as Father was dead" (Murry, ed., *Letters,* 389).

The virtuosity of the story lies in the treatment of time and point of view. The omniscient author has no voice, but as in "Prelude" (to which Mansfield declared this one akin in form), is free to speak through any consciousness in the story. Most of the narrative unfolds through the mind of one sister or the other, but sometimes their likeness is stressed by a composite viewpoint, which can split with ease. As they talk of sending their father's watch to Benny in Ceylon, Josephine points out that it would be carried by runners, for both a black messenger. "Josephine's black man was tiny; he scurried along glistening like an ant. But there was something blind and tireless about Constantia's tall, thin fellow, which made him, she decided, a very unpleasant person indeed" (473). Their minds move together, separate in a manner that individualizes them, and join again. Consistently Constantia seems to know what Josephine is talking about, even when she introduces a subject abruptly. It is an evidence of their long, secluded life together, but it is also technically necessary in order to ready the reader for the climatic penetration into their longings, which are differently expressed but complementary.

Time seems at the mercy of these minds wandering into the past and vaguely into fantasies of the future, but it is, in fact, well under Mansfield's control. Though a week is impressionistically described, sections 6 through 12 take place on the last day—the Saturday after the colonel's death. Section 5 occurs on Thursday, while sections 2 (where its time becomes specific) and 4 are on the Saturday, respectively morning and afternoon. Only the first two sections and part of the third are generalized to suggest typical behavior during the week and thus to contribute the aura of bemused muddle, which is the essential tone of the women through whose minds most of the events are seen.

During these segments of present story time there are recollections of the past: the colonel's single eye glaring in death, Mr. Farolles's offer of "a little Communion" (468), Cyril's remarkable communication at tea, efforts to lay traps for the haughty maid Kate—all are ridiculous. Visions of the future are fantasies: the colonel furious about his own funeral bills, the runner taking the watch to Benny, the plans for cooking should Kate be dismissed. The vague, erratic circling in the minds of these women reveals not only their history and characters but also their disability, their absurdity. The total view accords with their abandonment of any possible change. The most revealing statement is the opening sentence of the story: "The week after [the colonel's death] was one of the busiest weeks of their lives" (463). That it should be so is the mark of their utter deprivation.

With neither compassion nor humor, "The Fly" emerges as Mansfield's starkest view, her bitterest and almost her final cry against corruption. At its most obvious level, the events of the story are slight. The boss enjoys the admiring visit of an enfeebled old friend until the deaths of their sons are recalled. Alone, unable to summon the self-pity he has mistaken for grief, he diverts himself by tormenting to death a fly, but he is further depressed by this activity. He is clearly sadomasochist. The satisfactory docility of the remembered son,[4] coupled with his guilt in looking at the boy's picture, leads one to suspect that his treatment of the fly reflects similar though less extreme behavior toward his son. He no doubt bullied the boy as he now bullies Macey and Woodifield. But the feeling persists that there must be more than the immediately perceived meaning in this much-explicated story.

Mansfield's notebooks, letters, and short stories are sprinkled, from 1918 on, with images of flies. It might be merely a visual description of a baby, as in "The Voyage"; of little boys dressed in black; or an account of her own illness, as in the letters of 1918 and 1919.[5] She had felt herself to be like a fly "dropped into the milk-jug & fished out again . . . still too milky and drowned to start cleaning up yet" (*Letters,* 2:8), and she had imaged Jonathan Trout, who felt himself a victim of unknown forces, as an insect that could have been a fly (Berkman, 194). It is not unlikely, then, that her own position in a losing conflict with ill health, destiny, an insensitive father,[6] and even, since the fly struggles in the ink, the battle to meet short story deadlines are reflected at the biographical level in the story.

But if biographical readings are often dubious, how much more so for a writer who avowedly projects her being, for the literary moment, into every person or beast she describes. The meaning of the story may be more deeply plumbed within the fictional frame.

The likeness between old Mr. Woodifield and the boss goes beyond their mutual loss of sons in the war.[7] Neither has been to Belgium to visit the graves; both have apparently suffered deeply from grief; but most significantly, both, when the thought of these deaths crosses their minds, quickly forget.[8] It is not just doddering old Woodifield who cannot remember that he intended to mention his daughters' visit to their sons' graves, but the final sentence of the story emphasizes a similar lapse on the part of the robustly healthy boss: *"For the life of him* he could not remember" (602; my italics). There is multiple meaning here: not remembering seems to the boss to support his own vitality, but to restore the life of his son, he would not be able to remember, because he does not really wish to have that "stern-looking" young soldier take over the business and mastery that he himself possesses with such pleasure. He also does not wish to come, as has his near-double Woodifield, under the tutelage of his junior.[9]

The condition of Woodifield, which the boss enjoys in others but fears in himself, is clearly defined from the beginning, when he is compared to a baby in a pram. His voice is a weak piping. Others govern his behavior and even dress him. But if he is a baby, the boss is little more: in the imagery of Mansfield, he "rolled in his office chair, stout, rosy, five years older" (597). He is a boy, a greedy boy,[10] whose new office furniture suggests treacle and sausages. And like a boy, he torments the fly. In his good health he is no more manly than old Woodifield, but he is far more disturbing.

Through such a portrait of what Mansfield had called in 1919 "the Boss Omnipotent" she flung her final defiance in his teeth. From the beginning her stories had asked, "What is it all for?" and the answer had only been "how *stupid*" (61–62). She was without belief in any superior force governing the affairs of men, but her protest here is made clear in anthropomorphic terms. The force, she would say, that creates and then destroys is materialistic, gross, motiveless. There is no transcendence, no glimmer of the ideal in the process of bloom and decay. But worse, there is immaturity, lack of depth, in the cruel, destructive pattern.

The hope implicit in flowering intensifies the desolation of destruction. All the relationships of the story demonstrate this point. The boss has treated his son as he treated the fly, alternately assisting and encouraging, then crushing. In the rearing of boys such behavior is typically called "making a man of him," but the portrait of the man challenges the boss, so his grief at the loss is false. His treatment of Woodifield and Macey splits the two aspects of the bully's behavior or the pattern of life.[11] To Woodifield the boss is benevolent, giving him a taste of whiskey.[12] Macey he has bullied until the old office worker is reduced to subhuman behavior, a doglike personality. "Look sharp" are the boss's words to both Macey and the fly (602).

But the feelings of the boss are involved in his behavior. He enjoys the visit of the enfeebled old man and the slavish nervousness of Macey. His empathy with the fly connects him symbolically with these men. The fly "cowed" is Macey; "timid and weak," it is Woodifield. Past grief has carried the boss through these stages, compelling him to stand in relation to the forces of life as the fly stands to himself. The author has placed him in a cyclic progression, the meaning of which he unconsciously senses. The boy, Macey, Woodifield, the fly, and death are stages in a life sequence in which the boss has too many positions. His position as prime mover he enjoys; his identity with all of those who move toward death he prefers to forget.[13] A frightening reminder of his low degree is the "grinding feeling of wretchedness" which occurs when he kills the fly (602). It is an unwitting enactment of his own position. He destroys, but he is destroyed. On one level it is a statement about the sadomasochist; on another, a last description of the incomprehensible life pattern which feeds on its own destruction.

Something of the mature Mansfield's methods can be seen in the original manuscript of "The Voyage," which in August 1921 interrupted for four days her work on "At the Bay." It is one of the *Sphere* stories, written quickly, on commission from Clement Shorter. She was working on it 11 August 1921, when she wrote that it was "difficult," that she didn't know how she would write it (*Journal,* 259). The Newberry MP, Notebook 5 contains the first draft with corrections, dated at the beginning "14 viii 1921."

Told entirely through the viewpoint of the child Fenella, it relates her boat trip to Picton and her "grandma's" house. Understated suggestiveness deftly replicates the mind of a child who observes but does not interpret, a form which provides a model for many modernist and contemporary stories to follow. Fenella's awareness of tension as her father sees her off with grandma, increases to fear of abandonment when he can neither look at her nor reply to her question, "How long am I going to stay?" Then he gives her the remarkable (to the young child) sum of a shilling, and her anxiety crescendoes: "She must be going away forever! 'Father!' cried Fenella." The ship pulls away from the wharf. Water rushes between while the child "strained" to see her father until he disappears, and she can only return to her grandma. The dramatic orchestration of fear dissipates in grandma's "bright nod" and apparent loss of sadness (527).

The mystery of that sadness is soon dispelled, indirectly, through overheard remarks of the ship's stewardess. Her observation of the passengers' black clothing returns them to the mournful mood. Later she specifies the loss in her remark "Poor little motherless mite!" (531).

After a short sleep they awake to a dawn landing. Fenella, trembling with cold, wonders: "Oh, it had been so sad lately. Was it going to change?" (531). Her answer is nuanced in the story's last sentence as she meets her grandpa and "he looked at [her] so merrily she almost thought he winked at her" (533).

The story has usually been disregarded as a minor work, but may have been too subtle for its audience. The constraints of the viewpoint call upon the reader's acute attention and emotional imagination. The technical courage implicit in this demand by the self-excluding writer is the hallmark of a mature Mansfield story and epitomizes what she established as modernism in fiction. All details and their overtones must be taken into account. The significance of prosodic and emotional rhythms and other verbal sounds usually identified with poetry unfolds in a array of sense perceptions and muted symbolic imagery. Mansfield's insistence on selfless objectivity set a mode which would eventually initiate schools of critical theory.[14]

The manuscript reveals something of the problem Mansfield finally dealt with. As we learn from a list of prospective stories in her October 1921 *Journal,* she sometimes generated a story from a key phrase, which she intended to embed in her text. She worked from 27 September to 3 October to create a list of eight stories intended for her next book. The location would alternate between London and New Zealand. For the sixth story, "Widowed," which she never completed, she noted, besides the setting and a detail of costume, the phrase "Married or not married." The entry for the eighth story reads "N.Z. At Karori: 'The little lamp. I seen it.' And then they were silent" (*Journal,* 268). This will become the resonating ending of "The Doll's House."

The intention and consequent "difficulty" of "The Voyage" was similarly to use a phrase which would establish the mood and probably provide closure for the story. Notebook 5 reveals four attempts to locate the intended phrase. In the manuscript the story begins on f. 14r with a title, "That Voyage," under which is written "Going to Stay with her Grandma," an announcement of the key phrase. All efforts to use it are on f. 25r (see reproduction opposite p. 105).

In the first version Fenella hears her grandma talking to her grandpa in the next room; she pets the cat, then sees the gloomy moral poem in "a big black frame" on the wall. The quoted poem is immediately followed by "She was in Grandma's house." The sentence is crossed out and replaced with "Half an hour later she was in bed—in granma's [*sic*]

house." This too is crossed out, and Mansfield again tries to end the story:

> The blind tapped [crossed out]. A far away rooster called. The cat sprang off the table [inserted above the line: *On the wall*]. There was a big white text in a big black frame. Fenella read [space left here to quote the poem.]
>
> And she put down her bag sausage & the swan necked umbrella. She was in grandma's house.

"And she put down . . . umbrella" is crossed out for "Then the door opened and grandma came in. [*A claw got in the cat's ear. And now for a treat* crossed out.] Welcome dear Fenella [above line] she said to your [above line] grandma's house!" At this point the entire page is crossed out, and on the opposite page (f. 24v) Mansfield begins the new version with the entry into grandpa's room and then revises to nearly the final form of the story. The originally intended phrase has been abandoned at different locations four times.

Why? Because none of the efforts to use it had ended the story with the clear implication that finally remains. Grandpa challenges the gloomy text, shifting the emphasis from "GONE FOR EVER!" back to the "Golden Hour / Set with Sixty Diamond Minutes." As Fenella has hoped, the sadness is gone.[15] Neither the excitement of being in grandma's house nor the addition of "Welcome" to the phrase unambiguously expresses pleasure; but if any use of the phrase did, it would result in overstatement. Grandpa's possible wink is a tentative observation, but it clearly emphasizes the necessary change in tone which resolves Fenella's tension and so ends the story. The writer's objectivity offers only a hint, leaving interpretation to the reader. This avoidance of closure, sometimes called "negative" or "degree zero" ending,[16] is one of the narrative techniques Mansfield did much to establish in the English short story.

The *Sphere* stories are usually dismissed as a group, largely because they were written under pressure to fulfill a contract with a middlebrow periodical and were printed with disappointing illustrations. A misleading cue was provided by Mansfield herself, when she wrote Lady Ottoline Morrell on 24 July, "I don't believe they are much good." She explains, "[T]oo simple. It is always the next story which is going to contain everything, and that next story is always just out of reach" (Murry, ed., *Letters*, 2:390). Of course, she cannot write seriously about art to the amateur Ott. But the letter, though it says all of the *Sphere* stories are finished, is inaccurate. On that date, of those printed in *Sphere*, Mansfield had completed only "Mr. and Mrs. Dove" and "An Ideal Family."[17] If in July she had finished four other stories, she apparently judged them too poor for publication. Since we cannot know what these hypothetical stories were, we cannot know whether Murry published them later or whether Mansfield destroyed them.

In fact, she usually wrote rapidly and by 1921 put herself under pressure, not only to pay her medical bills but mainly because, aware of "the nearness of death and its inevitability" (*Journal,* 272), she wished to create a valid oeuvre while she had time. She pressed on to discover forms and techniques that approached an ideal of art she valued to the end.

Mansfield's *Journal* of that period reflects an aspiring artist's continual dissatisfaction with what has just been created. Of "Mr. and Mrs. Dove" she comments, ". . . [A] little bit made up . . . not inevitable . . . not quite the kind of truth I'm after." Of "The Ideal Family" she writes, " . . . [D]idn't get the deepest truth out of the idea. . . . I know so much more." But she thinks it's better than "Dove." These are *Journal* entries of July (256–57). In September, after finishing "The Voyage" in the midst of work on "At the Bay," she notes, "But my idea, even of the short story, has changed rather, lately—." On 14 October she calls "The Garden Party," not yet finished, "moderately successful . . . somehow, in the episode at the lane, scamped." Three days later the story is better than "At the Bay" "but not good enough either" (*Journal,* 262, 266–67). We need not trust this typical impatience of the artist seeking improved modes of expression, but clearly Mansfield took the *Sphere* stories as seriously as her important "At the Bay."

Indirectly her discoveries and aspirations at this time appear in her 12 November 1921 letter to William Gerhardi about his manuscript draft of *Futility.* Generously she encourages the young writer, but on his chapter 11 she writes, "[Y]ou falsify the tone. . . . [Y]ou begin to tell us what we must feel about them, what the sight of them . . . really meant, and that's not necessary. One feels they are being 'shown off,' rather than seen" (Murry, ed., *Letters,* 2:417). These remarks reflect what she means by objectivity and avoiding the personal, keeping her personal self out of her fiction.

Her stories, though often reflecting, as for any artist, her own experiences, are not records of her life and have been greatly misused as such by her biographers. While still an adolescent she had decided to "use" but to alter in her writing what she experienced. Alpers (340, footnote) thinks "The Voyage" commemorates the third anniversary of her mother's death because Mansfield began it 11 August. Perhaps. But her

mother died when she was 30, not when she was a child. And Alpers
(4–5) surmises that her first voyage to Picton was made at the age of six
months, considerably younger than Fenella. The story is not about what
really happened, and it is not about Mansfield. It imagines feelings she
or any other little girl might have had making such a trip after a mother's death. And it uses memories of her two grandmothers, of traits of
men she has known (including her father), and of voyages to Picton. Out
of such materials writers have always written.[18]

Katherine Mansfield was not a philosopher, though, among others, the
philosopher Bertrand Russell found her mind interesting. Unlike some
modern short story writers, she neither followed nor formulated a system
of thought; nor did she wish to. Her desire was to achieve purity of vision:
to see clearly herself in order to transmit truth to the reader. Like Conrad,
she wanted to make the reader *see*. But like Chekhov, she had no program;
she made no recommendations; she presented problems but no solutions.
To her the essential problem was just that absence of explanation.

Probably—at least, there is no evidence to the contrary—she never
heard of existentialism, but her most consistent observation is of the
absurdity that dominates life. So it rings out in her mature stories: isolation, unnecessary and often self-imposed; the capacity for life absurdly
wasted; motiveless destruction which involves self-destruction. Her sympathy is limited for individuals who victimize themselves; in her view of
the helpless she escapes the sentimentality of her early work to achieve a
detachment that does not exclude comic treatment. She regretted her
negation; she mitigated it in her affirmations of beauty; but she could
never deny what she saw: in the end, usually too soon, beauty faded, joy
bore an undertone of sadness, love was inadequately realized, order was
an ebb and flow that involved disorder.

Shortly after her thirty-fourth birthday, sure that her attitude had
been wrong and her selection of materials falsely controlled, she ceased
to write and entered the Gurdjieff Institute for the Harmonious
Development of Man at Fontainebleau. She hoped to "get into that real
living simple truthful *full* life" that she had groped for in her notebooks.
According to Murry and to conversations reported by Orage, the institute did "purify" her, and she expected to begin writing again, a new
kind of affirming story,[19] but death intervened.

Her spiritual and artistic malaise is common to the early twentieth
century but rises also from her personal experience. The conventional
family barely humored her youthful creativity, love failed her early, then

her body betrayed her with ill health that haunted her adult years. Educated and aspiring beyond her suffocating colonial environment, she risked loneliness and penury to discover herself as an artist. Romantically Pateresque and epigrammatically Wildean in youth, she alternated between sentiment and satire, but as Kaplan has shown, the techniques of Mansfield's 1908 letters to Garnet Trowell already foreshadow her impact on modernist fiction. Kaplan concludes that "by her early twenties [Mansfield's] style was refined and perfected, reflecting a merging of experimental techniques (symbolism, impressionism, internal mono- logue, stream of consciousness, cinematic visual effects, etc.) with femi- nist insights, protest, and self-assertion" (Kaplan, 17).

Kaplan has brilliantly detailed the relationship of Mansfield's intellec- tual and sexual development in a period of immense social change and experimentation to her emergence as a dominant shaper of modernist fiction. This analysis effectively argues that Mansfield's final achieve- ment surpasses what she had mocked as the posturing of "those dark young men": "If we consider modernism as Katherine Mansfield tried to shape it, we find a modernism stripped of its tendency toward objectifi- cation, stripped of either its apotheosis or its debasing of the feminine. It is a modernism full of doubts, questionings, and terrors, but it is also a modernism that leaps beyond both the despair of the 'waste land' and the hierarchical, traditional escapes from it posed by many of her male contemporaries" (Kaplan, 219).

Austin M. Wright's analysis of what distinguishes the traditional from the modern short story in America reads like a description, as he is aware, of a Mansfield work. In form he finds the modern story reduced in magnitude, tending toward the static. In the much-diminished plot, reversal, often muffled, has come "an illuminating moment in which the important constant in the static situation asserts itself." Dramatic effect is increased, in that the reader of the increasingly complex form often understands more than the protagonist. Wright explains the result:

> These tendencies—the reduction of magnitude of action and the refine- ment of complexity—make possible the development of richer and more delicate effects within the confines of short-story length. . . . By using the small action, the illuminating episode, as a unifying principle, the writers of the twenties reduced the amount of activity or incident necessary to bring their stories to completion. Thus they had more scope for the devel- opment of character and thought. . . . [In this] attempt to sharpen and

concentrate the focus of the short story . . . they brought [it] much closer
to the nature of the lyric poem.

He finds the significant forerunners in this mode to be Chekhov, Joyce,
and Katherine Mansfield, and he notes their kinship in depicting "social
disintegration and emotional isolation."[20]

Likewise Erich Auerbach (482–83, 487–88) sees the "distinctive characteristics of the realistic novel of the era between the two great wars . .
.—multipersonal representation of consciousness, time strata, disintegration of the continuity of exterior events, shifting of the narrative
viewpoint"—as symptoms of a confused, declining society. Yet despite
the frequent "impression of hopelessness" and "something hostile to the
reality which they represent," he finds in the exploitation of the "random
occurrence" and in its rendering in depth the discovery of the literary
matter "which is comparatively independent of the controversial and
unstable orders over which men fight and despair." His analysis of these
techniques and attitudes in Virginia Woolf's *To the Lighthouse* could as
easily have resulted from a study of Mansfield's "The Daughters of the
Late Colonel."

More recently Clare Hanson reflects on the modernist view of character as neither fixed nor knowable. She sees in short fiction "a sense of
external personality as an ever changing, infinitely adjustable 'envelope'
surrounding the real self, neither ego nor id, but a transcendent
essence. . . . [T]he task of the writer [is] to express his sense of the tensions between external and internal identity and to reveal moments
when one most nearly approaches awareness of his inner self."[21]

Kaplan (179) finds here a strong influence by Walter Pater, to whom
"personality is something fashioned, something aesthetic from the start."
Fullbrook (17) contrasts Mansfield's "deep but resisted desire to believe
in a continuous self" as an approximate acceptance of "Bergsonian ideas
common among other modernist writers—in what Joyce called 'epipha-
nies' and Virginia Woolf 'moments of being.' " She finds in Mansfield,
though "attracted to the possibility of a unified self . . . , a final hanging
back. And it is this hesitation, this honest uncertainty in the face of
desire and need, that finally makes Katherine Mansfield, at times, one of
the toughest and darkest of modernists."

Mansfield shared technical kinship with Joyce in that "almost every
detail of a given fiction will have a metaphoric as well as a narrative
dimension" and belongs to "a composed and harmonious whole"
(Hanson, *SS,* 127). This suggestiveness reflects their symbolist heritage,

their youthful reading of Wilde, Pater, and Symons. Both share as well the modernist narrative tendency to set up expectations and follow them with "moments of disappointment or denial" (Hanson, *SS,* 63)

But Mansfield differs from the male modernist in her projection into the being of her subjects, whether apples, ducks, or people. She disliked the self-conscious, melancholy, sometimes arrogant airs of "these dark young men" (*Letters,* 2:318), whose pretensions she mocked in "Je ne Parle pas Français" and "Bliss." She did not stop, as so many despairing male modernists did, in a wasteland. From this deadend she was saved by insistence on "ineffability as a necessary component of the modernist aesthetic gesture" (Kaplan, 219).

Serious writers do not always self-consciously set out to reflect the age or to relieve it of its conflicts by some artistic formulation. They are part of a complex which they define only in artifacts. Their effort is, by the act of integration in creation, to relieve, if anyone, themselves. Except in rare instances, usually when the artist has become critic and/or teacher, they have remained inarticulate or inaccurate in declarations about the larger significance of their work. The discreet makers simply stand by what they have made.

Thus Mansfield—always dissatisfied with her work and at the end reaching out for some new breakthrough to greater "reality"—without a systematically stated critical theory, reflected, as was inevitable, her era and provided technical solutions for writers who faced and would face similar problems. That her work was a dominant influence in the development of the modern short story is not debatable, though it may be an accident of time and publication history.

Her most important collections, *Bliss* and *The Garden Party,* were published on both sides of the Atlantic in the first three years of the 1920s. The extent of interest in her work in 1923, the year of her death, is reflected in the need for three printings of *The Dove's Nest* by Knopf in the first three months of the book's existence. There is no doubt that Murry exploited the interest created by her death. He managed to keep her before the public in his journal the *Adelphi,* and abroad in the *Yale Review,* with two years of posthumous publication. By 1930 he had brought out eight volumes of writing that Mansfield never intended for print. Again, when Knopf issued a complete collection, *The Short Stories of Katherine Mansfield* (September 1937), a second printing was needed by November, a fifth by 1950. Reprints continued in the 1980s. The stories have never gone out of print. Berkman (2) has described the development of Mansfield's "legend" as "a wash of sentiment that inundated the periodicals of England, America, and France." But despite the intellectual and aesthetic inadequacy of Mansfield's initial reception, her stories circulated. She was read widely, apparently by many who would also write.

It is difficult to insist on specific influences among writers of this period because they were all attacking similar materials and working out similar solutions. But as they found their attitudes and technical approaches in one another, they were no doubt encouraged. Coming first were the much-published Mansfield and James Joyce. The tale of the nine years it took before timid publishers and recalcitrant printers would issue *Dubliners* is twice-told. The edition of 1914 published by Grant Richards scarcely sold 500 copies in its first year (Ellmann, 412). In December 1916 the work appeared in the United States, and H. L. Mencken, urged by its publisher, B. W. Huebsch, had published two of the stories in *Smart Set* (Ellmann, 395). The Modern Library edition of 1926 made the stories more widely available. The kinship between Joyce's "epiphany" concept of the short story and the focus of Chekhov and Mansfield on moments of revelation has been described by Berkman (159–160), who suggests a plausible chain of influences—Turgenev, Chekhov, Mansfield, and Turgenev, George Moore, Joyce—to account for the coincidence. Though he is never included in what has become the customary triumvirate, Sherwood Anderson, whose *Winesburg, Ohio* appeared in 1919, importantly influenced the development of the American short story.

Bearing in mind that influence is partly a matter of who came first and that the short story was under intense social pressures which brought about the changes so well worked out in Mansfield's fiction, it perhaps enriches one's view of the literary stream to look at a few relationships that existed.

Virginia Woolf and Katherine Mansfield were interested in one another's work by 1917. This was the year Mansfield wrote happily, "[W]e have got the same job, Virginia, and it is really very curious and thrilling that we should both . . . be after so very nearly the same thing." (*Letters*, 1:327) In this year too the Woolfs arranged to bring out "Prelude" under the imprint their newly founded Hogarth Press; they did so in 1918.

The friendship suffered in the following years from separations due to Mansfield's illness and consequent absences abroad. Sometimes she was too ill to visit or write, and Woolf felt rebuffed by these failures. She was also momentarily stung by Mansfield's cautiously slighting review of *Night and Day,* though, rethinking Leonard's suggestion that Mansfield probably looked for flaws in her rival's writing, Woolf recognized that she was similarly guilty. When she found herself "looking for faults," she decided not to review Richardson's *Interim.* She suspected such envy rose from "an instinct for self-preservation. . . . If she's good then I'm not" (*VW Diary,* 1:314–15) Earlier, in June 1919, Mansfield had favorably reviewed "Kew Gardens." This contrast may have stimulated the experimental direction in which Woolf continued in *Monday and Tuesday.*

Despite ambivalence and doubts, when they could meet without the dampening presence of Murry—Woolf called him "mud-coloured and mute" (*VW Diary,* 1:265)—their open conversations and sense of community flourished.

Woolf's diary records her bafflement and desire. A few days after Mansfield married Murry, she called on Woolf, who wrote, "Katherine was marmorial, as usual. . . . As usual we came to an oddly complete understanding. . . . It's her love of writing I think. But she is off to Cornwall" (*VW Diary,* 1:150). The last sentence suggests disappointment that the conversations must be broken off. Mansfield apparently had concealed her precariously bad health. By August Virginia guessed that it might be hopeless (*VW Diary,* 1:177). She began a routine of weekly visits, which continued through the winter.

Lack of correspondence after Christmas raised Woolf's doubts again. On 18 February 1919, after the socially inept LM had phoned to cancel a scheduled visit, Woolf gnawed at the problem, trying unsuccessfully to deny her disappointment: "The question interests, amuses & also slightly, no very decidedly pains me. . . . I suppose that one of the conditions unexpressed but understood of our friendship has been precisely that it was almost entirely founded on quicksands" (*VW Diary,* 1:242–43).

Three days later Mansfield wrote, explaining that a treatment had incapacitated her and setting a new date for the following week. But afterward silence ensued until Woolf, giving the relationship a final chance, found Mansfield in the *Athenaeum* office on 22 March: " . . . the inscrutable woman . . . no sense of apologies due. At once she flung down her pen & plunged, as if we had been parted for 10 minutes, into the question of Dorothy Richardson; and so on with the greatest freedom and animation on both sides. . . . She's not the least of a hack" (*VW Diary,* 1:257–58).

On 12 July, shortly before Mansfield left England, Woolf reported on what she feared might be a last happy hour: "I like her more and more; & think we have reached some kind of durable foundation" (*VW Diary,* 1:291). When she heard of Mansfield's death, Woolf felt she had lost the only audience that could read her work.

Mansfield entries continue in the diaries and in letters until shortly before Woolf's suicide. On 15 January 1941 Woolf recalled Mansfield reading a bit of Joyce's *Ulysses*: " . . . the pages reeled with indecency. . . . She began to read, ridiculing: then suddenly said, But theres something in this: a scene that should figure . . . in the history of literature" (*VW Diary*, 5:353). This last entry unites the influential trio. In a little over two months Woolf was dead.

A letter Mansfield wrote in 1917 to Lady Ottoline about the garden at Garsington may have laid out a plan for Woolf's experimental "Kew Gardens." Surely Woolf showed it to Mansfield and received encouragement[22] which led her in the modernist direction. Impressionistic sketches, these slight performances published in 1919 and 1920, were useful in the development of techniques brought to full power in her following novels. The later short works collected posthumously in *A Haunted House* take the form of the modern short story. Of these, "The New Dress" seems to make deliberate reference to Katherine Mansfield's "The Fly." The Woolf story consists of the interior monologue of Mabel Waring, a transcript of her ordeal at a Dalloway party. Her anguish rises from social insecurity but is focused, for her, on the new dress which she herself has designed but has come to feel is unfashionable. She tries to comfort herself with a feeling that she is like the others, but the fly image she employs turns on her:

> We are all like flies trying to crawl over the edge of the saucer. Mabel thought, and repeated the phrase as if she were crossing herself, as if she were trying to find some spell to annul this pain, to make this agony endurable. . . . Now she could see flies crawling slowly out of a saucer of milk with their wings stuck together. And she strained and strained . . . to make herself see . . . all the other people there as flies, trying to hoist themselves out of something, or into something, meagre, insignificant, toiling flies. But she could not see them like that, not other people. She saw herself like that—she was a fly, but the others were dragonflies, butterflies, beautiful insects . . . while she alone dragged herself up out of the saucer.[23]

Throughout the party her mind dwells on the fly, Woolf's unifying image. Her final remark, as she leaves the affair, "Right in the saucer," expresses her feeling of self-derision. Near the end of the story there seems to be an explicit acknowledgment of the Mansfield source: "That wretched fly—where had she read the story that kept coming into her mind about the fly and the saucer?—struggled out" (*HH*, 57).

Similarity in the use of time divisions of a single day, the frames of "At the Bay" and *Mrs. Dalloway,* has been pointed out by Berkman (168–69). Again, the use of the sea as the unifying tonal image of that short story is surely related to the elaboration of the same device in *The Waves.* They begin at the same time of day and with very nearly the same sentence:

MANSFIELD: Very early morning. The sun was not yet risen. (263)
WOOLF: The sun had not yet risen.[24]

They conceive of the sea as "sleepy" and "a sleeper." Mansfield's opening section introduces a herd of sheep, as light begins to appear. With the rising of her sun, Woolf compares the waves to "turbaned warriors . . . who . . . advance upon the feeding flocks, the white sheep" (*Waves,* 54). Mansfield's fantasy of the sea's having covered the earth and its houses during the night is echoed in *The Waves:* "Tables and chairs rose to the surface as if they had been sunk under water" (*Waves,* 79). The notion is repeated to describe the end of the day: "As if there were waves of darkness in the air, darkness moved on, covering houses, hills, trees, as waves of water wash around the sides of some sunken ship" (*Waves,* 168). Their noon sequences describe a burning, pitiless, revealing sun. Of course, both are dealing with the same subject matter, though to different ends; both cultivated highly developed sensibilities as a means to expression. Still, the impressions of "At the Bay" must have left some record, at least, in Woolf's unconscious mind, to bear fruit in her later novels.

The important point is not that Virginia Woolf repeats specific images and structural devices used by Katherine Mansfield. The two women display a kinship in craft as they think about how to treat their materials: the extent of the narrator's knowledge, as well as what to make available to and what to require of the reader; the increase of dramatic quality in the use of particular details; the avoidance of narrative passages; the increase of immediacy in the use of interior monologue and the freedoms that device allows in dealing with time. Each reflects the uncertainties of her age: neither will, neither feels that she should, reach more than implicit conclusions in her writing. Like Henry James, they "create their readers," requiring that they grasp inferences and attain for themselves the revelations to which stories lead. In this kinship of craftsmanship—no matter how motive, style, or attitude toward the subject may differ—lies these women's likeness to James Joyce, to the writers of the 1920s, and to many followers in modern fiction. Their difference is that they are consciously feminists.[25]

Because in the 1920s and after, many writers, exploring the short story medium with similar needs for expression, moved in kindred lines of development, it is easy to find a kinship with Katherine Mansfield in many instances. The more subjective women writers, such cultivators of sensibility as Elizabeth Bowen and Eudora Welty, are immediate candidates. Awareness of the genealogy appears in Ruth M. Vande Kieft's study of Welty:

> Since the central meaning is to be conveyed by indirection, all of these writers [Chekhov and Mansfield] have developed their own methods of shaping their material with minute care. They invest with maximum significance each detail, each small piece of dialogue, narration, or description; and they endow each metaphor with an emotional resonance comparable to that of poetic metaphor. This care and subtlety in formal construction, this lyrical and poetic richness and psychological complexity, ask for corresponding sympathetic qualities in the reader, as does the fiction of James Joyce, Virginia Woolf, and Katherine Anne Porter. All of these writers have prepared the way for Miss Welty's writing and also for our reading with pleasure and discernment her particular kind of fiction.[26]

Bowen's family membership is laid to the zeitgeist by Sean O'Faolain: "[T]he prime technical characteristic of her work, as of other modern women writers, such as Virginia Woolf, is that she fills the vacuum which the general disintegration of belief has created in life by the pursuit of sensibility."[27] She herself had early noted the resemblance of her work to Mansfield's.

But here we are pulled up short with a warning proper to all historians too nearsightedly intent on tracing relationships. Bowen has written, "I read *Bliss* when I had completed the first set of my stories which were to make *Encounters*—then admiration and envy were shot through by a profound dismay: I thought: If I ever am published, everybody will say I imitated her. I was right: this happened."[28]

Whatever her influence, Mansfield stands finally on the longevity of her work. In it there was immaturity, as there must be for those who begin in youth and never reach old age. There were potboilers, as there must be for those who need the money the pen can earn. But even the early, heavily satirical stories of *In a German Pension* can still evoke laughter, to say nothing of recognition, from anyone who has boarded for a few weeks with strangers. The observation from the first was of reality, which the overreaching of youthful antagonisms cannot dispel. Mansfield could see, and she taught her reader to see.

And to hear. Talk is a large part of the subject in the first stories—the interminable, banal chatter of the German pensioners, who steadily expose their ignorance, greed, chauvinism, and selfishness. Even with the excessive comments of an undisciplined narrator, the talk reveals more of Mansfield's disdain than she overtly states. Already a deft selection of materials is her means of communication; indirection is her chosen method. She had an ear for distinctions among speakers, and she did not lose it. There is a terseness in the language of nobility not matched by the German bourgeoisie, whether romantic or practical. A structural nuance in the dialogue reminds the reader too that this is not the speech of the English.

In fact, the male notion that Mansfield's style is all too frequently the same for all her characters, a style which reflects her own feminine voice—"fluttery, gossipy, breathless"[29]—disregards a large portion of her work and misreads her intention. The early naturalistic New Zealand characterizations explored the possibilities of dialect with acumen. The speech of the ignorant is not forgotten in the monologues of the lady's maid and Ma Parker or the conversation of Mrs. Stubbs and Alice in "At the Bay." Mansfield children always speak with their imaginative, concrete directness. The "effeminate" speech patterns and diction of Raoul Duquette and lesser members of his band, such as Eddie Warren and Bobbie Kane, are unmistakable. More substantial is the tone of Stanley Burnell and his counterpart John Hammond, yet it is quite different from the understated worldliness of the men of "The Escape" and "The Man Without a Temperament."

Mansfield dissects some fluttery women, but the voice of Moira Morrison or Isabel of "Marriage à la Mode" is not her voice; nor, unless in memory of her adolescence, do the many young girls speak for her. Kaplan astutely notes that when the voice in a Mansfield short story is overtly feminine, the writing is deliberately artificial and frequently satirical. The writer "*sees* through the stylistic devices to their origins in women's oppression or self-delusion" (Kaplan, 158–59; Kaplan's italics). The vague disconnection of the colonel's daughters is unlike any of the rest. If there is any alliance between the thought processes and speech of her characters and Mansfield, it probably is reflected in such wary protagonists as Vera in "A Dill Pickle" and the unnamed woman of "Psychology." In her mature work Mansfield herself does not appear. The voice she selects is chosen for its meaning within the story.

Her characters are memorable for the moments of discovery in which they speak, aloud or to themselves. Usually the emphasis is on a larger concept than the description of an individual. "I seen the little lamp" concentrates for the reader any number of affirmative stands. In Bertha Young's final observations—" 'Oh, what is going to happen now?' . . . But the pear tree was as lovely as ever and as full of flower and as still"— the wonder and terror of life are juxtaposed. A larger will to isolation than John Hammond's is exposed when he tells himself that "[T]hey never be alone together again."

As Elizabeth Bowen has pointed out, the short story is not the medium for full character development, and Mansfield did well in perceiving this limit of the form.[30] Thus if her characters are to take on depth, it is usually in the New Zealand stories, where the same people are met again and again. The reader's intimacy with Stanley Burnell, Kezia, Beryl, and even the aloof Linda increases until it is as if Mansfield had written the novel she hoped for when she began work on "Prelude."[31] Her depth is evident in the sympathy extended to all these individuals, so very much at cross-purposes.

Stories of kindred content also overlay one another, the awareness of one increasing the understanding of another. As with most writers, certain themes, subjects, and images preoccupy Mansfield. Her study of isolated women ranges from the nerviness of Monica Tyrell through the valiant sensitivities of Miss Brill to the rebellious desire for "life" of Beryl and the subversive independence of Kezia. At a tangent to this subject are the variety of married women who are also alone: the hysterical, compensating Bertha Young; the shallow Isabel, torn between the values of bohemia and her husband; the withdrawn Linda Burnell; Janey Hammond, the stranger; and the uneasily dependent invalid of "The Man Without a Temperament."

From the beginning Mansfield's portrayal of women reflects the depth of her feminism. She is critical of Rosabel's wishful imaginings fed by her escape into sentimental romance reading, but the exploited shop-girl's pathos is also evident in her need for such escape. The German pension is filled with stereotypically gendered women, either sexually oppressed victims (Kaplan, 129) or those more subtly abused by their acceptance of, even pride in, identities defined by their husbands' occupations. The English boarder, originally named Kathleen, defies their standards as she refuses to marry, submit, and bear children.

Mockery of oppressive male fatuity varies from a minor theme in "At the Bay" and "The Life of Ma Parker" to the major thrust of "Mr.

Reginald Peacock's Day" and "The Stranger." It becomes a crushing menace in "The Fly."

Mansfield's critical attitude remained constant from girlhood. In 1908 she enthusiastically wrote her sister Vera, "[D]o read 'Come and Find Me' by Elizabeth Robins . . . All this suffragist movement is excellent for our sex" (*Letters,* 1:47). In her journal she added, "a clever, splendid book. . . . We [women] are firmly held with the self-fashioned chains of slavery. . . . they . . . must be self-removed" (*Letters,* 1:36–7).

Early in her cohabitation with Murry she angrily objected to his casual expectation that she alone was responsible for housekeeping: "Yes, I hate hate HATE doing these things that you accept just as all men accept of their women. . . . & you calling (whatever I am doing Tig—isn't there going to be tea? Its five o'clock.) As though I were a dilatory housemaid!" (*Letters,* 1:126).

Of overbearing businessmen fathers, one of Mansfield's so-called obsessive subjects,[32] it is a long distance from "Bottlenose" in her *Scrapbook* (50) to the harried disciplinarian of "Sixpence." Relationships of such men with their families are not always those of the irascible colonel; they may reflect the puzzled fatigue of old Mr. Neave. The ego of Stanley Burnell is very different from, much more humane than, the ego of Reginald Peacock. Different again is that of John Hammond, the self-made stranger. While the boss, unlike but as abstract and ominous as the figures of the early "Child-Who-Was-Tired," is intricately as much symbol as man, though the man is still wretchedly, frighteningly human.

There is, perhaps, a greater sameness in the excited, half-formed adolescent young women who reach out impatiently for a romantic image of "life," but Laura after the garden party can rise to an incoherent insight. And the young men, as they grow a little older, can look back upon themselves with jaded sophistication. The passionate innocent of "Something Childish But Very Natural" may be on the way to his "poison" in "Mr. and Mrs. Dove." The protagonist of "The Escape" has avoided the life-denying losses of "The Man without a Temperament."

Considering all this variety—and there is more—it is odd to read of the limitations which Mansfield's experience imposed on her subject matter. Every writer is so limited. What did Tolstoy know beyond the Caucasian wars, his serfs, the society he moved in, and a little history? Has not William Faulkner mined the provincial Mississippi county that was apparently his most informing experience? It is not scope that matters to literature but depth. Clarence Buddington Kelland has probably exploited a hundred widespread scenes with the same combinations of "characters," the same stereotyped plot, yet most readers will not recognize his name. Katherine Mansfield wrote of a small part of New Zealand, of London literary life, of Paris and the Riviera, of children, servants, and boardinghouse inmates. But the limit to her treatment of what she saw was only the limit of time: she died before she could write all her stories. Perhaps because her social and geographical range was small, her perception intensified.

Critics are fated by time and perhaps biology to become swiftly out of date. Politically alert women, at least, will find Kate Fullbrook close to the mark: "[Mansfield's] stories demand to be read as unremittingly critical accounts of social injustice grounded in the pretence of a 'natural' psychological and biological order that is disproved by the experience of consciousness. Image and plot, symbol and idea—all the elements of her fiction function as protests against any ideology of fixture and certainty. . . . [I]t is a body of work that incites to revolt through its critical appraisal of the circumstances Katherine Mansfield sees and records" (Fullbrook, 127–8).

Mansfield did not need many different scenes, for she used setting, like character, only to convey meaning. If she chose to describe a place, her work was vivid, specific in detail, but impressionistic. The labored blueprints of an Arnold Bennett were not necessary to the sense of location. A little data would give the tone of the experience to unfold there or characterize the person to whom the scene was meaningful. The significant items in John Hammond's hotel room are the bed and the dying fire, and they are enough to image his emotional disaster. Though the doll's house is described in great detail, illumination at last focuses around the little lamp. As the boss in "The Fly" points to his new office furniture, the reader sees, as well, the man and the quality of his avowed grief. Geographical juxtaposition of rich and poor in "The Garden-Party" emblems the simultaneity of frivolity and death; the sea, in many aspects, dominates the activities and meaning of "At the Bay." Mansfield kept under sharp control her capacity for poetic description, subordinating such passages always to her larger purpose. Even in stories which fail because of inadequate conception, her concern for form prevents lack of control.

This formal care, the restriction of meaning to the implicit, the awareness of paradox, and the resulting avoidance of dogma—in all these characteristics Katherine Mansfield is in the mainstream (and in advance of it) of modernist fiction. In her variety of treatment, depth of perception, and formal precision, but most of all in the continuing aliveness and immediate relevance of her stories, rests her claim to a place in literary history.

At such a position, however, she might have smiled. It was communication that mattered to this woman, who wrote so often of the inadequacy of human contacts. Sometimes she cared only for the appraisal of her friends: Murry, Walter De la Mare, George Santayana, a few others. Once, wondering about the public reception of a story, she wrote Murry, "Tell me if anybody says they like it, will you? . . . It's just a queer feeling—after one has dropped a pebble in. Will there be a ripple or not?" (Murry, ed., *Letters,* 628). One recorded moment of triumph came when she heard that the printer who set the type for "Prelude" had said of her manuscript, "My! but these kids are real!"[33] This was the reward, the goal achieved. She had told the truth, and someone had seen it. It was enough.

Notes

Chapter One

1. Rachel Allbright, in "Katherine Mansfield and Wingley," *Folio* 24 (Summer 1959): 23–29, has written of the cats in Mansfield's life.

2. *The Collected Letters of Katherine Mansfield,* ed. Vincent O'Sullivan and Margaret Scott, (New York: Viking Penguin, 1984, 1987, 1993), 3:226; hereafter cited in text as *Letters.*

3. Mansfield's childhood and adolescence were not the miserable experience highlighted by biographers and often critics, following the leads of the ridiculously unreliable, ambivalent Murry and the biography he controlled: Ruth Elvish Mantz, *The Life of Katherine Mansfield* (London: Constable, 1933). Anthony Alpers, because of his access to Mansfield family and acquaintances, is regarded as the official biographer. He wrote two versions: *Katherine Mansfield: A Biography* (New York: Knopf, 1954) and *The Life of Katherine Mansfield* (New York: Viking Press, 1980). His attitudes dominate not only later biographers but even topics for indexing *Letters.* His organizing viewpoint and commentary color otherwise useful objective information. (I make use of the objective data in the later book, cited hereafter in text as Alpers.) His principles of selection, undeclared, leave one wondering what has been left out. Too frequently he regards the short stories as transcripts of fact. His followers, Jeffrey Meyers (*Katherine Mansfield* [New York: New Directions, 1978]) and Claire Tomalin (*Katherine Mansfield: A Secret Life* [New York: Knopf, 1988]) are equally reductive and untrustworthy. Tomalin sometimes displays, as her preface promises, womanly understanding, but her reasoning and treatment of sources are flawed: too often a hypothesis on one page becomes a fact on the next. Useful accounts of the problems are Ann Else, "From Little Monkey to Neurotic Invalid: Limitation, Selection, and Assumption in Anthony Alpers, *Life of Katherine Mansfield,*" *Womens Studies International Forum* 8, no. 5 (1985): 497–505; Dennis McEldowney, "The Multiplex Effect: Recent Biographical Writing on Katherine Mansfield," *Ariel* 16 (October 1985): 111–24; and C. K. Stead, "Mrs Bowdenhood," *London Review of Books,* 26 November, 1987, 24–25. Murry's skewing of the primary documents is detailed most recently in Ian A. Gordon's edition of Mansfield's *The Urewera Notebook* (London: Oxford University Press, 1978), 14–20. Gordon, 12–13, 20–24, and Gillian Boddy, *Katherine Mansfield: The Woman and the Writer* (New York: Penguin Books, 1988), 5, deny the unhappy childhood "tradition." The above sources are hereafter cited in text by surnames.

4. Boddy, 5, confirms the offense to Butts, who recalled Kathleen "as enjoying playing tricks on teachers—on one occasion challenging her" for her opinion on Free Love.

5.   On the matter of Mansfield's lesbianism, which occasionally attracts apparently modish attention, certainly sometimes she preferred women to men. So many women, as well as men, do, that such an object choice seems completely natural. In fact, people who don't prefer men have no choice but to prefer women, if they like anyone at all. Was Mansfield bisexual? We all are unless taught a particularizing gender role. As Rachel Blau Du Plessis writes, "The oedipal crisis is a social process of gendering that takes 'bisexual, androgenous,' libinally active, and ungendered infants and produces girls and boys . . . within the rules of the sex-gender system of its society" (*Writing Beyond the Ending: Narrative Strategies of Twentieth-Century Women Writers* [Bloomington: Indiana University, 1985], 35–36, a sensible, contemporary discussion of Freudian theory). Many, with varying degrees of social and psychological success, resist this gendering process. The sooner we abandon categories, perhaps useful to social "scientists" and religious fanatics but biased by sexual politics and economics, the more clearly we may be able to contemplate the various nuances of individual human behavior.

6.   *Journal of Katherine Mansfield,* ed. J. Middleton Murry (London: Constable, 1954), 103; hereafter cited in text as *Journal.*

7.   Described in her *Urewera Notebook.*

8.   Tomalin, 64, asserts that Mansfield was already pregnant by Garnet Trowell, which motivated the marriage.

9.   The list includes peritonitis, pleurisy, rheumatism, and tuberculosis. The generally accepted belief that gonorrhea caused her rheumatism rests on scant medical evidence: a medical history Mansfield gave Dr. Bouchage in 1921, which reads parenthetically, "very likely from gonococcal origin," and a report of something said by the aging Ida Baker. The original document appears to have been lost or destroyed. Tomalin, 75–78, who ignores "very likely," discusses the disease in detail. Alpers, 115–16, accepts the disease, though, paradoxically, he doubts Baker's "allegation."

10.   Gordon, 17–18, contains his most recent description of Murry's misleading assembly of *The Scrapbook of Katherine Mansfield* (New York: Knopf, 1940), hereafter cited in text as *Scrapbook,* and two versions of *Journal*—1928, enlarged in 1954.

11.   James Moore, *Gurdjieff and Mansfield* (London, Boston, and Henley: Routledge & Kegan Paul, 1980), provides a sympathetic account of Mansfield's retreat to and death at La Prieure.

12.   Alpers, 388, describes how Murry, parsimonious to the end, "forgot" to pay the bill for Katherine's funeral, with the result that she was buried in "common ground," a pauper's grave. When her father learned of this in 1929, he sent his son-in-law, Charles Renshaw, to have the grave moved to perpetual care.

13.   *The Diary of Virginia Woolf,* ed. Anne Olivier Bell and Andrew McNeillie (New York and London: Harcourt Brace Jovanovich, 1977–84), 1:265; hereafter cited in text as *VW Diary.*

14. *The Letters of Virginia Woolf*, ed. Nigel Nicolson and Joanne Trautman (New York and London: Harcourt Brace Jovanovich, 1975–80), 3:59.

15. Clare Hanson, *The Critical Writings of Katherine Mansfield* (New York: St. Martin's, 1987), 6; hereafter cited in text as Hanson, *Crit*.

16. *The Letters of Katherine Mansfield*, ed. J. Middleton Murry (New York: Knopf, 1929), 2:417; hereafter cited in text as Murry, ed. Letters. His one-volume edition, *Katherine Mansfield's Letters to John Middleton Murry, 1913–1922* (New York: Knopf, 1951) is similarly cited without volume numbers.

17. Sydney Janet Kaplan, *Katherine Mansfield and the Origins of Modernist Fiction* (Ithaca, N.Y., and London: Cornell University, Press, 1991), 182.

18. Richard Ellmann, *James Joyce* (New York: Oxford University Press, 1959), 218, 364; hereafter cited in text. Lack of comment in Mansfield's writing suggests that she was unfamiliar with Dubliners. She eventually knew *Portrait of the Artist* and *Ulysses*.

Chapter Two

1. Alpers, who in 1954 (130-32) concluded that the story was "an indisputable plagiarism", in 1980 (Alpers, 111–12) engaged in an ambiguous but hostile straddle. Apparently because plagiarism is thematically central for Tomalin, she provides, in appendix 2 (261–72), documents of the *Times Literary Supplement* correspondence-debate, which ran from 19 October through 21 December 1951. In the course of this jeu d'esprit, Sylvia Berkman reviewed the scholarship, Alpers called the story "an exercise," and A. E. Coppard finally mounted a sensible writerly defense; all reprinted by Tomalin.

2. Ronald Sutherland, "Katherine Mansfield: Plagiarist, Disciple, or Ardent Admirer?" *Critique* 5 (Fall 1962): 70, 72, 75.

3. Anton Tschechoff, *Ein Bekannter Herr: Humoristische Geschichte,* trans. Wladimir Czumikow (Jena: Diederichs, 1910).

4. Renata Poggioli, *The Phoenix and the Spider* (Cambridge, Mass.: Harvard University Press, 1957), 110.

5. During this period two other stories were printed: "Mary" (*Idler,* March 1910) and "A Fairy Story" (*Open Window,* December 1910). See B. J. Kirkpatrick, *A Bibliography of Katherine Mansfield* (Oxford: Clarendon Press, 1989), for a detailed listing of Mansfield publications, manuscripts, films, discography, etc.

6. Paul Selver, *Orage and the New Age Circle* (London: Allen & Unwin, 1959), 17, 26, 46.

7. As the letters of that spring reveal, Mansfield was hard-pressed for money, so much so that by April, one day after angrily rejecting excisions from "Je ne Parle pas Français," she felt compelled to reconsider, trusting Murry's judgment for nearly the last time: "If you agree to what they say—why then all's well (and I [DO] want the money)" (*Letters,* 3:274).

8. *The Short Stories of Katherine Mansfield* (New York: Knopf, 1950), 91; page references to stories are hereafter cited in text; editorial material hereafter cited in text as *SS*.

9. Anton Chekhov, *The Black Monk and Other Stories,* trans. R. E. Long (London: Duckworth, 1903); hereafter cited in text.

10. Kate Fullbrook (*Katherine Mansfield* [Bloomington and Indianapolis: Indiana University Press, 1986], 39–40) emphasizes "doubling" to suggest parallels between the Child and both her mother and the baby. These similarities develop the theme of "oppression of women and children who live outside the protection of patriarchal law."

11. See Andrew Wachtel, "Resurrection à la Russe: Tolstoy's *The Living Corpse* as Cultural Paradigm," *PMLA* 107 (March 1992): 261–73. Tolstoy, Wachtel notes, decided to write *Living Corpse* as a corrective after he "became incensed" upon seeing Chekhov's *Uncle Vanya* (271 n2).

12. Marie Bashkirtseff, *The Journal of a Young Artist: 1860–1884,* trans. Mary J. Serrano (New York: Cassell, 1889), 142: "*Sic transit gloria Ducis.*" Anti-German feeling is also evident, as on 138–39.

13. Mansfield was in Bavaria between June 1909 and January 1910.

14. Fullbrook provides acute feminist commentary for several of these. See especially 43–51 on Mansfield's description of the "sadistic edge in the schooling [of little girls] into gender" (49) in the patriarchal family.

15. Mansfield's later evaluation of this sort of "cleverness" is evident in "Je ne Parle pas Français," when Duquette congratulates himself on such phrase-framing.

16. This remark probably reflects not only Mansfield's response to her miscarriage in Bavaria but also the influence of Beatrice Hastings, an assistant editor of the *New Age,* who, according to Philip Mairet, in *A. R. Orage: A Memoir* (London: 1936), 51, had written an article pleading that the state protect women from the "horrors of giving birth." Sometime before May 1911 Hastings may have assisted Mansfield in obtaining an abortion (Alpers, 122-24). Murry, in *Journal,* 44, doubts that there was an abortion.

17. "The Breidenbach Family in England" was unsigned, and apparently Murry remained unaware of it. The ascription is Berkman's (212, n. 6). Also in the *New Age* at this time appeared the uncollected "Festival of the Coronation."

18. The whole scene is clearly New Zealand, not Germany. See Berkman, 216, n. 26.

19. Leonard Woolf, *Beginning Again, 1911–1918* (London: Hogarth Press, 1964), 203–4.

20. Alpers, 99, notes that some of the names were those of Worishöfen villagers.

21. Pamela Dunbar of the University of Warwick, in her insightful presentation "Complex Characters: The Narrator and Her Fellow Cure-Guests from the First-person German Pension Sketches," at the Newberry Library

Mansfield Centennial Symposium, 8–10 September 1988, examined the narrator's persona; typescript hereafter cited in text.

22. Probably still a private joke, best appreciated by New Zealanders and others of Commonwealth extraction.

Chapter Three

1. J. Middleton Murry, *Between Two Worlds: An Autobiography* (London: Jonathan Cape, 1935), 184; hereafter cited in text as *B2W*.

2. Clare Hanson and Andrew Gurr, *Katherine Mansfield* (London and Basingstoke: Macmillan, 1981), 39, describe the structure as arising "mainly from . . . leitmotif [the color red] and prolepsis [the first appearance of the rifle] . . . a rhythmical structure analogous to that of a Post-Impressionist painting"; hereafter cited in text.

3. These are the German names, which appeared in *Rhythm*. They were changed in Murry's posthumous collection of the stories to Helen and Dr. Malcolm. The Binzer family, clearly that of "A Birthday," became Carstairs. Murry dates the story 1910.

4. *Rhythm*, August 1912. The fears and nightmares are Murry's, as he recalled them in *B2W*, 16, 24, but apparently he only saw children beaten when he peeped through a fence at his boisterous neighbors or observed canings at school (*B2W*, 21, 39).

5. *Rhythm*, June 1912, 35. She is kinder to Strindberg, who attracts and repels her; hilarious, in a skit written with Murry, on a play by J. M. Synge (*Rhythm*, August 1912, 120–21).

6. *Rhythm*, June 1912, 37–39.

7. The story is dedicated to Anne Estelle Rice, a Fauve painter whose work often appeared in *Rhythm*.

8. Cherry Hankin (*The Confessional Stories of Katherine Mansfield* [(London: Macmillan, 1983], 68–70) has no doubt of this. She may overstate her case regarding Mansfield's proclivities and psychology; hereafter cited in text as Hankin.

9. Alpers, 164, says the story "hints" of Mansfield's relationships with Murry and William Orton. Our interpretations differ considerably.

10. Alpers, 167, notices this in a different context.

11. Cherry Hankin, ed., *Letters between Katherine Mansfield and John Middleton Murry* (New York: New Amsterdam Books, 1992), 15; hereafter cited in text as *Letters btwn*. I use this text for Murry letters and, when possible, Mansfield's after April 1920, the end month of *Letters, 3*. When Hankin is lacking, I have used the less scholarly editions by Murry (See chapter 1, n16).

12. Murry published three segments, labeling two "unposted letter" (*Journal*, 25–29). These two are reproduced in *Letters*, 1:149–50, though only the notebook remains.

13. Paul Fussell, *The Great War and Modern Memory* (New York and London: Oxford University Press, 1975), 119, 118.

14. I find Kaplan's reading (118–22) of the story as a feminist statement inconsistent. The plot displays "the vulnerability" of a naive child, not "of women in a world dominated by male power." And while Kaplan takes Berkman to task for "blaming the victim," she concludes that "a woman becomes a conspirator in her own destruction when she incorporates the ideology of her oppressor into her own identity." It is such a conclusion that is involved, at this early stage of her development, in Mansfield's mockery. Kaplan also does not resolve the question she raises about point of view, which I take as a flaw, preliminary to Mansfield's later mastery of multiple viewpoints.

15. Hanson and Gurr, 45–47, describe this as "the most purely symbolist of her stories to this date." They analyze the symbolic use of music, wind, and sea.

Chapter Four

1. *SS*, Murry's introduction, vii.

2. The first-person narrator of the 1915 version of "The Wind Blows" was changed to third person for 1921 publication in *Bliss*.

3. Erich Auerbach, *Mimesis*, trans. Williard A. Trask (Garden City, N.Y.: Doubleday, 1957), 471–74; hereafter cited in text.

4. Mansfield complained to Murry that Woolf ignored the war in *Night and Day* (*Letters*, 3:82). Her sardonic *Athenaeum* review of 26 September 1919 scorns W. B. Maxwell's *A Man and His Lesson*, in which the declaration of war saves the hero from suicide because of a marital dilemma: "Hurrah for August 1914! He is saved. Off he goes to be honourably killed. Off he goes to the greatest of all garden parties—and this time there is no doubt as to his enjoying himself" (Hanson, *Crit.*, 99).

5. *The Aloe*, ed. Vincent O'Sullivan (London: Virago Press, 1985), 42; hereafter cited in text as *Aloe*. This edition has been updated with Mansfield's manuscript corrections from O'Sullivan, ed., *The Aloe with Prelude* (Wellington, New Zealand: Port Nicholson Press, 1982).

6. Kezia's fear is more extensively imaged in *Aloe* and is very much like Linda's.

7. *Aloe*, 68–69, "And she dreamed that she [and her mother were] was caught up out of the cold water . . . [She saw her mother sitting quietly in the boat . . . it would be better if her Mother did not come]" Brackets enclose deletions from *Aloe* for "Prelude."

8. Kaplan, 169–87, provides a full discussion of "confession" versus objectivity in Mansfield's writing.

9. That Murry's mother was on Mansfield's mind when she wrote "Je ne Parle pas Français" is evident in her letter of 5 February (*Letters*, 2:57). She wrote, "After we are married, I want to know your mother differently. I cant before." Following Alpers (273), there is general agreement that Mansfield used Murry's abandonment of Margueritte and her own first meeting of Carco for

details of plot. Critics also follow Alper's suggestion that Duquette displays some of Mansfield's characteristics (e.g., Hankin, 161–62, who also notes the parallel of the 1912 visit to Paris, when Murry introduced Mansfield to Carco; Tomalin, 169–70; Kaplan, 185–87, adds an astute analysis of Duquette's opinions and style as parody of the modernist "dark young men" and the pseudo-avant-garde. But since Mansfield's avowed technique is to "become" whatever she writes about, her experience is likely to become part of any character.

10.   I have not seen a third variant, the Alexander Turnbull Library's Notebook 1, a 44-page pencil version with ink corrections. See Alpers, ed., *The Stories of Katherine Mansfield* (Oxford: Oxford University Press, 1984), for a brief description. Newberry Mansfield Papers cited in text hereafter as *MP*.

11.   In 1918 the exchange was 27 francs to £1, giving Mouse 540 francs. Traveling in January Mansfield was scandalized to pay 10.50 francs for hotel and dinner in Le Havre. She regarded a 12-franc room, evidently with meals, as expensive in Bandol. In wartime Paris she found a quiet, well-furnished room with dinner on the Place de Sorbonne for 6 francs (*Letters*, 2:4 and nn. 3, 7, 135). At that rate Mouse could have lived adequately for nearly three months. Mansfield, who kept careful accounts, would have known this.

12.   *Je ne Parle pas Français* (Hampstead: Heron Press, 1920), 25, 5.

Chapter Five

1.   In the summer of 1917 Mansfield and Murry began to think of finding a farmhouse to live in after the war ended. They named their fantasy "The Heron" in memory of her recently dead brother. After their May 1918 marriage they bought a house in Hampstead, which they named "The Elephant" (Alpers, 262–63, 280).

2.   Most immediately, LM's derided eating habits are probably latent in the dream. Mansfield's letters describing LM's assault on food are classics of comic satire. On 22 February 1918 Mansfield describes LM at lunch: "an Appetite which makes the hotel tremble, and after having downed the table-cloth glasses & spoons says what I miss are the puddings. . . . & then follows about 100 puddings. . . . She keeps them all flying in the air, like a conjuror & like a conjuror—eats em—" (*Letters*, 2:85). The theme frequently figures in letters to Murry.

3.   The connection with Margueritte was noted by Alpers, 273, and repeated by Meyers, 115; Hankin, 161–62; and Tomalin, 169. Kaplan (43–44) provides a subtle analysis of the Carco and Murry models, adding D. H. Lawrence to the complex and Mansfield's competitive position among male rivals for Murry's affection. I disagree with the view of Kaplan and Fullbrook (94) that Mouse is a victim. The best interpretive evidence is Murry's own in *B2W*, 463, 465. Of Mansfield's assertion that the story is "a tribute to love," he wrote, "Katherine meant this, and indeed it was only in part a self-deception, or a necessary illusion. It was true in the sense that only Love could feel and utter

the agony of Love's disaster." When he received the second part of the story, he was "dumb and numb, with pain. It hurt too much."

4. Over Mansfield's angry protests, Michael Sadleir insisted on censoring from "Je ne Parle pas Français" "Why should I be able to have any woman I want?" (*MP*, Box 1.26) when negotiating for Constable the publication of *Bliss*. (*Letters btwn*, 300, 302–3.) Both stories appear in that collection.

5. I am indebted to Professor Jan Lawson Hinely for the germ of this idea and even more for her painstaking, critical reading of additions to this second version of the book.

6. J. Middleton Murry, *Katherine Mansfield and Other Literary Portraits* (London: Constable, 1949), 9.

7. Hankin, 142–46, finds "lesbianism implicit in the symbolism" and relates the betrayal theme to Mansfield's possible jealousy of Lady Ottoline, but the February 1918 letters cited as evidence are not convincing. And, of course, Bertha, to whose consciousness the story is limited, cannot be trusted. There is no need to believe that Bertha "loved" Pearl Fulton or desired her husband. Bertha uses the word *love* too casually. The exposition introducing Pearl states, "Bertha had fallen in love with her, as she always did fall in love with beautiful women" (340–41). I agree with Judith S. Neaman ("Allusion, Image, and Associative Pattern: The Answers in Mansfield's 'Bliss,' " *Twentieth Century Literature* 32 [Summer 1986]: 249) that Bertha's "crush" reflects "the normal schoolgirl stage of maturation."

8. Mansfield may be displaying for her old friend D. H. Lawrence the use of phallic symbolism without his strident insistence, which she disliked so much.

9. Alpers, 318, cites Turnbull Notebook 25, p. 2. Cf. *Journal*, 208.

10. Cf. the sensitive explication of Donald W. Kleine, "Katherine Mansfield and the Prisoner of Love," *Critique* 3 (Spring 1960): 20–33. Kleine notes the wordplay on Salesby but interprets it differently.

11. The phrase comes from the analysis of structure, irony, and symbolism in Peter Thorpe's "Teaching 'Miss Brill,' " *College English* 23 (May 1962): 661–63.

12. I may be in slight conflict with Kaplan, 216, who sees the maintenance of gender roles as a subtext. Both Linda and Kezia are ambivalent about such constraints.

13. The time aspect of the story has been analyzed in Wallace Stegner, Richard Scowcraft, and Boris Ilyin, eds., *The Writer's Art: A Collection of Short Stories* (Boston: Houghton Mifflin, 1950), 74–77.

14. Fullbrook, 122–23, points out that the hat "changes Laura's politics in an extraordinary moment of conscience callousing over." She finds that Laura's easy character shifts "underscore Mansfield's insistence on the fragility of identity."

15. Leslie Moore, *Katherine Mansfield: The Memories of LM* (London: Virago Press, 1985), 158.

Chapter Six

    1.   In *MP* Box 2.21, the first draft of the story, the theme of the children's letters and Hammond's resentment of them has been squeezed in at the bottom of f. 5, a revision which intensifies the portrait of his selfishness.

    2.   The original manuscript first bore the title "The Interloper." The change to "The Stranger" marks an enlargement of meaning, possibly a discovery Mansfield came upon as she wrote the story.

    3.   Deleted in *MP,* Box 1.41, f. 30, is the statement that Josephine is 43; Constantia, 38.

    4.   *MP* Box 1.16, contains a passage in which the son resists working for his father. In this early draft the story is titled "The Manager," and throughout the manuscript "the manager" was originally written instead of "the boss."

    5.   Other references to flies are noted by Celeste T. Wright in "Genesis of a Short Story," *Philological Quarterly* 34 (January 1955): 91–96, and by Berkman, 193–94.

    6.   Wright, 91–96 and in "Mansfield's " 'The Fly,' " *Explicator* 12 (February 1954): Item 27; Willis D. Jacobs, "Mansfield's 'The Fly,'" *Explicator* 5 (February 1947): Item 32.

    7.   J. D. Thomas, in "Symbol and Parallelism in 'The Fly,' " *College English* 22 (January 1962): 261, points this out, but stresses their contrast, which is also evident. Notes 8–13 indicate similarities between my interpretation and those of others. Ultimately I agree with none.

    8.   Cf. R. A. Jolly, "Critical Forum: Katherine Mansfield's 'The Fly,' " *Essays in Criticism* 12 (July 1962): 338.

    9.   This play on the word *life,* Stanley B. Greenfield in "Mansfield's 'The Fly,' " *Explicator* 7 (October 1958): Item 2, says is Mansfield's "supreme achievement in the story. Time and life are too much for any man; . . . the past and its grief must yield."

    10.   Cf. R. A. Copland, "Critical Forum: Katherine Mansfield's 'The Fly.' " *Essays in Criticism* 12 (July 1962): 340.

    11.   Robert W. Stallman, in "Mansfield's 'The Fly,' " *Explicator* 3 (April 1945): Item 49, I believe, is the first critic to note that to the boss all three men are like flies and that the boss is himself alternately identified and not identified with the fly. Jolly (336–37) sees Woodifield, Macey, and perhaps the boss as flies. F. W. Bateson and B. Shahevitch, in "Katherine Mansfield's 'The Fly': A Critical Exercise," *Essays in Criticism* 12 (January 1962): 51, see a dual element of "sadistic tenderness" in the boss's relations with his son and Woodifield.

    12.   Cf. Bateson, 51.

    13.   I believe this analysis clarifies the meaning of the dualism suggested by Stallman, 49, and resolves the inconsistency found in this dualism by Berkman, 195. Cf. E. B. Greenwood, "Critical Forum: Katherine Mansfield's 'The Fly,' " *Essays in Criticism* 12 (July 1962): 346–47.

    14.   E.g., reader-response criticism, pioneered in Wolfgang Iser's *The Act*

of Reading (Baltimore: Johns Hopkins University Press, 1978), and further developed in his later books, most recently *The Fictive and the Imaginary* (Baltimore: Johns Hopkins University Press, 1992).

15.   Further study of f. 24v (which I leave to the pleasure of the intrigued reader) reveals slight revisions to limit language to a child's likely vocabulary and to increase visual specificity.

16.   See Wallace Martin, *Recent Theories of Narrative* (Ithaca, N.Y., and London: Cornell University Press, 1986), 84, and his analysis of "Bliss," especially 117, 138, 163–64, and 168.

17.   Meyers, 287–88 n31, provides a convenient dated list of stories from mid-July 1921 through 24 January 1922.

18.   Family names appear in the manuscript margins: f. 16, beside "my own brave son!" is written "Leslie Heron Beauchamp"; top of f. 17, "Mary Beauchamp." The hand and time of writing differs from that of the story.

19.   "Last Talks with Katherine Mansfield," *Century Magazine,* November 1924, 36–40.

20.   Austin M. Wright, *The American Short Story in the Twentieth Century* (Chicago: University of Chicago Press, 1939), 150, 266–67, 272.

21.   Clare Hanson, *Short Stories and Short Fictions* (New York: St. Martin's Press, 1985), 56; hereafter cited in text as Hanson, *SS.*

22.   Alpers, 250–52, believes that Mansfield's suggestions for a description of the garden at Garsington prompted Woolf to write "Kew Gardens."

23.   Virginia Woolf, *A Haunted House* (London: Hogarth Press, 1953), 50–51; hereafter cited in text as *HH.*

24.   Virginia Woolf, *The Waves* (London: Hogarth Press, 1953), 5; hereafter cited in text as *Waves.*

25.   Mansfield's feminism is the topic of Fullbrook's excellent book. Subscribing, as I enthusiastically do, to most of her analysis, I urge the reading of her book, rather than incorporating its details into mine. Kaplan, whose subject is modernism, deals effectively with Mansfield's rejection of male modernist attitudes.

26.   Ruth Vande Kieft, *Eudora Welty* (New York: Twayne, 1962), 180–81.

27.   Sean O'Faolain, *The Vanishing Hero* (Boston: Houghton Mifflin, 1957), 167.

28.   Elizabeth Bowen, *Early Stories* (New York: Vintage, 1951), viii.

29.   See H. E. Bates, *The Modern Short Story* (London: 1941), 129, and the response to his remarks by Berkman, 177–84. Kaplan (159–60) has more recently effectively challenged Bates.

30.   Elizabeth Bowen, introduction to Katherine Mansfield, *Stories* (New York: Vintage, 1960), xxi.

31.   Ian A. Gordon, ed., *Undiscovered Country: The New Zealand Stories of Katherine Mansfield* (London: Longmans, 1974), provides a collection of the New Zealand stories, supplemented by excerpts from journals, letters, and sketches;

but some of these stories could not be components of the family story. Kaplan, 101, argues that her feminist social critique, which entailed rejection of the marriage plot, mainstay of the conventional novel, may have forced Mansfield to the artistic breakthrough of her more experimental short story form.

32.   See the pioneering psychological studies of Celeste T. Wright, as listed in the Bibliography.

33.   Murry's introduction to *SS,* vii.

Selected Bibliography

PRIMARY WORKS

Fiction

Stories collected in each volume are listed in chronological order of publication. Only first editions are given.

In a German Pension. London: Stephen Swift, 1911.
　　(All stories previously published appeared in the *New Age,* as dated.)
　　　　"The Child-Who-Was-Tired," 24 February 1910.
　　　　"Germans at Meat," 3 March 1910.
　　　　"The Baron," 10 March 1910.
　　　　"The Luft Bad," 24 March 1910.
　　　　"At Lehmann's," 7 July 1910.
　　　　"Frau Brechenmacher Attends a Wedding," 21 July 1910.
　　　　"The Sister of the Baroness," 4 August 1910.
　　　　"Frau Fischer," 18 August 1910.
　　　　"A Birthday," 18 May 1911.
　　　　"The Modern Soul," 22 June 1911.
　　　　"The Advanced Lady" (not previously published).
　　　　"The Swing of the Pendulum" (not previously published).
　　　　"A Blaze" (not previously published).
Prelude. Richmond: Hogarth Press, 1918.
Je ne Parle pas Français. Hampstead: Heron Press, 1920.
Bliss and Other Stories. London: Constable, 1920.
　　　　"The Wind Blows," *Signature* 18 October 1915 (as "Autumn II").
　　　　"The Little Governess," *Signature* 18 October and 1 November 1915.
　　　　"Mr. Reginald Peacock's Day," *New Age* 14 June 1917.
　　　　"Feuille d'Album," *New Age* 20 September 1917 (as "An Album Leaf").
　　　　"A Dill Pickle," *New Age* 4 October 1917.
　　　　"Prelude," as above.
　　　　"Bliss," *English Review,* August 1918.
　　　　"Pictures," *Arts and Letters,* Autumn 1919.
　　　　"Je ne Parle pas Français," as above.
　　　　"The Man without a Temperament," *Arts and Letters,* Spring 1920.
　　　　"Revelations," *Athenaeum,* 11 June 1920.
　　　　"The Escape," *Athenaeum,* 9 July 1920.
　　　　"Sun and Moon," *Athenaeum,* 1 October 1920.
　　　　"Psychology" (not previously published).
The Garden-Party and Other Stories. London: Constable, 1922.
　　　　"Bank Holiday," *Athenaeum,* 6 August 1920.

"The Young Girl," *Athenaeum,* 29 October 1920.

"Miss Brill," *Athenaeum,* 26 November 1920.

"The Lady's Maid," *Athenaeum,* 24 December 1920.

"The Stranger," *London Mercury,* January 1921.

"The Life of Ma Parker," *Nation and Athenaeum,* 26 February 1921.

"The Singing Lesson," *Sphere,* 23 April 1921.

"The Daughters of the Late Colonel," *London Mercury,* May 1921.

"Mr. and Mrs. Dove," *Sphere,* 13 August 1921.

"An Ideal Family," *Sphere,* 20 August 1921.

"Her First Ball," *Sphere,* 28 November 1921.

"The Voyage," *Sphere,* 24 December 1921.

"Marriage à la Mode," *Sphere,* 31 December 1921.

"At the Bay," *London Mercury,* January 1922.

"The Garden-Party," *Saturday Westminster Gazette,* 4, 11, and 18 February 1922.

The Dove's Nest and Other Stories. London: Constable, 1923.

"The Doll's House," *Nation and Athenaeum,* 4 February 1922.

"Taking the Veil," *Sketch,* 22 February 1922.

"The Fly," *Nation and Athenaeum,* 18 March 1922.

"Honeymoon," *Nation and Athenaeum,* 29 April 1922.

"A Cup of Tea," *Story-Teller,* May 1922.

"A Married Man's Story," *Dial,* January–June 1923.

"Six Years After," *New Republic,* 28 March 1923.

"The Canary," *Nation and Athenaeum,* 21 April 1923.

(Other stories in this volume were unfinished at Mansfield's death and consequently were not previously published.)

Something Childish and Other Stories. London: Constable, 1924. (Also under the title *The Little Girl and Other Stories.* New York: Knopf, 1924.

"Late at Night," *New Age,* 10 May 1917.

"The Black Cap," *New Age,* 17 May 1917.

"Carnation," *Nation,* 7 September 1918.

"Sixpence," *Sphere,* 6 August 1921.

"Poison," *Collier's,* 24 November 1923.

"A Suburban Fairy Tale," *Adelphi,* December 1923.

"Something Childish but Very Natural," *Collier's,* 5 January 1924.

"The Tiredness of Rosabel," *Collier's,* 9 February 1924.

"See-Saw," *Adelphi,* July 1924.

(The following were not previously published.)

"An Indiscreet Journey."

"Spring Pictures."

"This Flower."

"Wrong House."

The Aloe. London: Constable, 1930.

The Aloe: With Prelude. Edited by Vincent O'Sullivan. Wellington, New Zealand: Port Nicolson, 1982.

Other Writing (Editions to which I have had access.)

The Collected Letters of Katherine Mansfield, vols. 1-3. Edited by Vincent O'Sullivan and Margaret Scott. Oxford: Clarendon, 1984, 1987, 1993. Excellent edition. Two more volumes expected by 1995.

The Critical Writings of Katherine Mansfield. Edited by Clare Hanson. New York: St. Martin's, 1987.

Journal of Katherine Mansfield. Edited by John Middleton Murry. London: Constable, 1954.

Gorki, Maxim, *Reminiscences of Leonid Andreyev.* Translated by Katherine Mansfield and S. S. Koteliansky. London: Hogarth Press, 1948.

Katherine Mansfield. Publications in Australia, 1907–1909. Edited by Jean E. Stone. Sydney, Australia: Wentworth Books, 1977. Early works published in E. J. Brady's *Native Companion.*

Katherine Mansfield's Letters to John Middleton Murry, 1913–1922. Edited by John Middleton Murry, New York: Knopf, 1951.

Letters between Katherine Mansfield and John Middleton Murry. Edited by Cherry Hankin, New York: New Amsterdam, 1988. Selected letters, an indispensable biographical tool.

The Letters of Katherine Mansfield. Edited by John Middleton Murry. New York: Knopf, 1929.

Poems of Katherine Mansfield. Edited by Vincent O'Sullivan. Oxford: Oxford University, 1988. A selection.

The Scrapbook of Katherine Mansfield. Edited by John Middleton Murry. New York: Knopf, 1940.

The Short Stories of Katherine Mansfield. Introduced by John Middleton Murry. New York: Knopf, 1950.

The Stories of Katherine Mansfield. Edited by Antony Alpers. New York: Oxford University Press, 1984. Eclectic selection, unfortunately called "definitive." Notes on manuscripts arouse curiosity.

"The Unpublished Manuscripts of Katherine Mansfield." Edited by Margaret Scott. *Turnbull Library Record* 3–6, 12 (1970–74, 1979).

The Urewere Notebook. Edited by Ian A. Gordon. New York: Oxford University Press, 1978.

Periodicals

Adelphi 1 (June 1923–May 1924); 2 (June 1924–May 1925).
Athenaeum 4 April 1919–11 February 1921.
Blue Review 1 (May–July 1913).

New Age 6, n.s. (November 1909–April 1910); 7 (May–October 1910); 9
      (May–October 1911); 10 (November 1911–April 1912); 18 (November
      1915–April 1916); 21 (May–October 1917).
Rhythm 1–2 (Summer 1911–March, 1913).
Signature 1 (4 October–1 November 1915).

Juvenilia

"Enna Blake." *The High School Reporter* (Wellington), 1898.
"A Happy Christmas Eve." *The High School Reporter* (Wellington), 1898.
"The Pine Tree, the Sparrow, and You and I." *Queen's College Magazine* 22
      (1903).
"Die Einsame." *Queen's College Magazine* 23 (1904).
"Your Birthday." *Queen's College Magazine* 23 (1904).
"One Day." *Queen's College Magazine* 25 (1905).
"About Pat." *Queen's College Magazine* 25 (1905).
"Vignettes." *Nature Companion* (Melbourne), October 1907.
"Silhouette." *Nature Companion* (Melbourne), November 1907.
"In a Café" *Nature Companion* (Melbourne), December 1907.
"The Lonesome Child." *Dominion* (Wellington), 6 June 1908. A poem.
"Why Love is Blind." *New Zealand Freelance,* 20 June 1908.
"Study: The Death of a Rose." *Triad* (New Zealand), July 1908.
"The Education of Audrey." *Evening Post* (Wellington), 20 January 1909.
"November." *Daily News* (London), 3 November 1909. Poem, first named
      "October."
"The Fairy Tale." *Open Window* (London), December 1910.
"Floryan Nachdenklich." *Dominion)* (Wellington), 3 March 1913. Poem.
"Old Tar." *Westminster Gazette* (London), 25 October 1913, reprinted in the *New
      Zealand Times,* 11 December 1913.
"His Ideal." Alexander Turnbull Library MS. Papers 119. Unpublished.
"Juliet." See Scott's edition. Previously unpublished.
"My Potplants." Alexander Turnbull Library MS. Papers 119. Unpublished.
Scott, Margaret, ed. "Brave Love." *Landfall* 26 March (1972); 3–29. Previously
      unpublished, written January 1915.

Editing and Manuscript Description

The major collections of Mansfield manuscripts are in the H. Ransom
Research Center University of Texas; the British Library, London; the
Newberry Library, Chicago; and the Alexander Turnbull Library,
Wellington, New Zealand. There are a few items in the Berg Collection,
New York Public Library; the Huntington Library, San Marino,
California; the McMaster University Library, Hamilton, Ontario,
Canada; the Stanford University Library, Palo Alto, California; and the

Assumption University Library, Windsor, Ontario, Canada. Indications are that Murry's editing created the Mansfield image he preferred; hence critical interpretations related to Mansfield biography, as many have been, need revision based on new textual information. The most productive work has gone forward in the Turnbull Library, where Margaret Scott has been editing unpublished manuscripts since 1969 and is coediting a new edition of Mansfield's letters for Oxford University Press. The Turnbull Library is preparing a microfilm edition of the Mansfield papers, also edited by Margaret Scott.

Gordon, Ian A. "The Editing of the Katherine Mansfield Manuscripts" *Landfall.* 13 (March 1959): 62–69. A detailed description of the manuscripts behind the *Journal* versions of 1927 and 1954 and the 1939 *Scrapbook,* first exposure of Murry's editorial distortions.

Morris, Maude E. "A Katherine Mansfield First: *The Lonesome Child.*" *Turnbull Library Record.* 4 (October 1971): 103.

Scott, Margaret. "The Extant Manuscripts of Katherine Mansfield" *Etudes Anglaises* 26 (Oct.–Dec. 1973): 413–19. A description of holdings at Turnbull and other libraries, public and private.

———. "More KM Manuscripts." *Turnbull Library Record.* 7 (May 1974): 18. A bequest of letters from Mansfield's sister, Vera Macintosh Bell.

———. "Note on 'Brave Love'." *Landfall* 26 (March 1972): 29–30.

———. "The Unpublished Manuscripts of Katherine Mansfield." *Turnbull Library Record.* 3 (March, 1970): 4–28. *Juliet*

———. "The Unpublished Manuscripts of Katherine Mansfield. Part II." *Turnbull Library Record.* 3 (November 1970): 128–36. Six short pieces from Notebook 1, 1906.

———. "The Unpublished Manuscripts of Katherine Mansfield. Part III." *Turnbull Library Record.* 4 (May 1971): 4–20. The rest of notebook 1 and *Toot,* an incomplete play in MS. Papers 119 (two drafts).

———. "The Unpublished Manuscripts of Katherine Mansfield. Part IV." *Turnbull Library Record.* 5 (May 1972): 19–25. A 28 page notebook, maybe written 1909 in Germany and/or the end of 1914. Report on photocopies of two untraced manuscripts of "Brave Love," given by Ida Baker.

———. "The Unpublished Manuscripts of Katherine Mansfield. Part V. *The Laurels.*" *Turnbull Library Record.* 6 (October 1973): 4–10. The outline and first scene of a Christmas play written for a party at Garsington Manor on 29 December 1916, acted by KM, Murry, Lytton Strachey, Brett, Carrington, Bertrand Russell, and Maria Nys.

————. "The Unpublished Manuscripts of Katherine Mansfield. Part VI. Two *Maata* Fragments." *Turnbull Library Record.* 7 (May 1974), 4–14. Parts of the *Maata* novel begun in 1913.

————. "The Unpublished Manuscripts of Katherine Mansfield. Part 7." *Turnbull Library Record* 12 (May 1979): 11–28.

Waldron, Philip. "A Katherine Mansfield Poem Printed Incomplete." *Notes and Queries.* 21 (January 1974): 365–66.

————. "Katherine Mansfield's Journal." *Twentieth Century Literature.* 20 (January 1974): 11–18. Detailed description of Murry's "extreme carelessness" as editor.

SECONDARY WORKS

Bibliographies

Bardas, Mary Louise. "The State of Scholarship on Katherine Mansfield, 1950–1970." *World Literature Written in English* 11 (April 1972): 77–93. An annotated checklist, including dissertations.

Kirkpatrick, B. J. *A Bibliography of Katherine Mansfield.* Oxford: Clarendon, 1989. Meticulous description of publications, manuscripts, films, plays, recordings, etc.

Meyers, Jeffrey. "Katherine Mansfield: A Bibliography of International Criticism, 1921–1977." *Bulletin of Bibliography and Magazine Notes* 34 (April–June 1977): 53–67. More than 635 books, articles, and important reviews in 14 languages, attesting to worldwide interest.

————. Katherine Mansfield: A Selected Checklist." *Modern Fiction Studies* 24 (Autumn 1978): 475–77. Updates his 1977 bibliography in a special Mansfield issue of *MFS*.

Biography and Background

Alpers, Antony. *The Life of Katherine Mansfield.* New York: Viking, 1980. Generally considered "definitive" but unfortunately marred by male bias, probably influenced by the aging Murry. See Else, McEldowney, and Webby.

Bashkirtseff, Marie. *The Journal of a Young Artist.* Trans. Mary J. Serrano. New York: Cassell, 1889. Youthful reading.

Benet, Mary Kathleen. *Writers in Love: Katherine Mansfield, George Eliot, Colette, and the Men They Lived With.* Boston: G. K. Hall, 1984. Compares relationships three strong women had with weak men.

Bernikow, Louise. *Among Women.* New York: Harmony Books, 1980. Sympathetic account of alternating envy and respect between Mansfield and Virginia Woolf, 126–41.

Boddy, Gillian. *Katherine Mansfield: The Woman and Writer.* New York: Penguin, 1988. Life in New Zealand context, non-Alperian, many photographs reproduced, selected stories with commentary.

Brown, Sally. " 'Hundreds of Selves': The British Library's Katherine Mansfield Letters." *British Library Journal* 14 (Autumn 1988): 154–64. Account of writer's adaptation to various correspondents: LM, Koteliansky, Schiffs, etc.

Carswell, John. *Lives and Letters: A. R. Orage, Beatrice Hastings, Katherine Mansfield, John Middleton Murry, S. S. Koteliansky, 1906–1957.* New York: New Directions, 1978. Two Mansfield milieus.

Cassavant, Sharron Greer. *John Middleton Murry: The Critic as Moralist.* University: University of Alabama Press, 1982. Murry's criticism examined in the context of his life.

Crone, Nora. *A Portrait of Katherine Mansfield.* Elmscourt and Ilfracombe, Devon: Arthur H. Stockwell, 1985.

Else, Ann. "From Little Monkey to Neurotic Invalid: Limitation, Selection, and Assumption in Antony Alpers' *Life of Katherine Mansfield." Women's Studies International Forum* 8 no. 5 (1985): 497–505."

Hankin, Cherry A., ed. *The Letters of John Middleton Murry to Katherine Mansfield.* London: Constable, 1983. A selection from the Turnbull Library, annotated with Mansfield's answering letters and background. Appendix lists all unpublished Turnbull letters and telegrams.

McEldowney, Dennis. "The Multiplex Effect: Recent Biographical Writing on Katherine Mansfield." *Ariel* 16 (October 1985): 111–24. Reviews all biographies from Mantz to the second Alpers; also Hankin, *Confessional Stories,* and *Letters* of JMM. Finds contradictions and confusion.

Meyers, Jeffrey. *Katherine Mansfield: A Biography.* London: Hamish Hamilton, 1978. Flawed reasoning, misuse of sources. See Webby ("soap opera") and McEldowney.

Moore, James. *Gurdjieff and Mansfield.* London and Boston: Routledge & Kegan Paul, 1980. Sympathetic account of Mansfield's residence and death at Fontainebleau. Sardonic account of Murry's "career" before and after.

Moore, Leslie. *Memories of LM.* London: Virago, 1985. Recollections of the aging, faithful "wife." Quotes Mansfield letters.

Murry, John Middleton. *Between Two Worlds: An Autobiography.* London: Jonathan Cape, 1935. Mansfield enters the life at chapter 14.

Selver, Paul. *Orage and the "New Age" Circle.* London: Allen & Unwin, 1959. Describes the *New Age* ambience.

Stead, C. K. "Mrs. Bowdenhood." *London Review of Books,* 26 November 1987, 24–25. Review of Tomalin, challenging some "facts" and assumptions.

Tchekhoff, Anton. *The Black Monk and Other Stories.* Trans. R. E. C. Long. Freeport, N.Y.: Books for Libraries, 1970. Reprint of 1903 edition Mansfield may have read.

Tomalin, Claire. *Katherine Mansfield: A Secret Life.* New York: Knopf, 1987. Sources misused, oversimplification. Sometimes displays the feminine understanding advertised in the preface. See Stead.

Webby, Elizabeth. "Katherine Mansfield: Everything and Nothing." *Meanjin* 41 (June 1982): 236–43. Discussion of Murry's editing of Mansfield. Reviews of Meyers and Alpers.

Woolf, Virginia. *The Diary of Virginia Woolf,* vols. 1–5. Edited by Anne Olivier Bell. New York: Harcourt Brace Jovanovich, 1977–84.

———. *A Haunted House and Other Stories.* London: Hogarth Press, 1953.

———. *The Letters of Virginia Woolf,* vols. 2–6. Ed. Nigel Nicolson and Joanne Trautman. New York: Harcourt Brace Jovanovich, 1976–80.

———. *To the Lighthouse.* New York: Harcourt, Brace, 1927.

Critical Studies

No explications of single stories.

Anderson, Walter E. "The Hidden Love Triangle in Mansfield's 'Bliss.' " *Twentieth Century Literature* 28 (Winter 1982): 397–404.

Baldeshwiller, Eileen. "Katherine Mansfield's Theory of Fiction." *Studies in Short Fiction* 7 (Summer 1970): 421–32. Analysis of comments on formal and aesthetic problems in letters, journals, and reviews.

Banks, Joanne Trautman. "Virginia Woolf and Katherine Mansfield." In *The English Short Story, 1880–1945: A Critical History,* ed. Joseph M. Flora, 57–82 Boston: Twayne, 1985. A fine appreciation of both. Discusses the relationship, femininism, themes, form, influence.

Berkman, Sylvia. *Katherine Mansfield: A Critical Study.* New Haven Conn.: Yale University Press, 1951. The first scholarly study.

Blanchard, Lydia. "The Savage Pilgrimage of D. H. Lawrence and Katherine Mansfield: A Study in Literary Influence, Anxiety, and Subversion." *Modern Language Quarterly* 47 (March 1986): 48–65. Lawrence anxious, Mansfield subversive.

Brown, Constance A. "Dissection and Nostalgia: Katherine Mansfield's Response to World War I." *Centennial Review* 23 (Summer 1979): 329–45. Oversimplified but begins an approach.

De Salvo, Louise A. "Katherine Mansfield and Virginia Woolf's Revisions of 'The Voyage Out.' " *Virginia Woolf Miscellany* 11 (Fall 1978): 5–6. Mansfield's influence.

Du Plessis, Rachel Blau. *Writing beyond the Ending: Narrative Strategies of Twentieth-Century Women Writers.* Bloomington: Indiana University Press, 1985. Feminist and psychological study of narrative.

Fullbrook, Kate. *Katherine Mansfield*. Bloomington: Indiana University Press, 1986. Challenges reductive, biographically oriented criticism; argues strongly that Mansfield is a feminist writer.

Gubar, Susan. "The Birth of the Artist as Heroine: (Re)production, the *Kunstlerroman* Tradition, and the Fiction of Katherine Mansfield." In *The Representation of Women in Fiction,* Edited by Carolyn G. Heilbrun and Margaret R. Higgonet, 19–59. Baltimore: Johns Hopkins University, 1983. Debatable relationship of creativity to maternity.

Hankin, Cherry A. *Katherine Mansfield and her Confessional Stories*. London and Basingstoke: Macmillan, 1983. Insistent though speculative psychological analysis of stories, system unspecified. In the preface Freud is mentioned twice, and Jung references are taken from Magalaner.

Hanson, Clare. *Short Stories and Short Fictions*. New York: St. Martin's Press, 1985. An astute account of the genre.

Hanson, Clare, and Andrew Gurr. *Katherine Mansfield*. London and Basingstoke: Macmillan, 1981. Close reading of many stories.

Leech, Geoffrey N., and Michael H. Short. *Style in Fiction: A Linguistic Introduction to English Fictional Prose*. London and New York: Longmans, 1985. "An Example: Katherine Mansfield," 126–33, analyzes a single sentence to exemplify linguistic methods.

McLaughlin, Ann L. "The Same Job: Notes on the Relationship between Virginia Woolf and Katherine Mansfield." *Virginia Woolf Miscellany* 9 (Winter 1977): 11–12.

———. "The Same Job: The Shared Writing Aims of Katherine Mansfield and Virginia Woolf." *Modern Fiction Studies* 24 (Autumn 1978): 369–82.

Martin, Wallace. *Recent Theories of Narrative*. Ithaca, N.Y.: Cornell University Press, 1986. Analysis of Mansfield's "free indirect style," 136–40.

Neaman, Judith S. "Allusion, Image, and Associative Pattern: The Answers in Katherine Mansfield's 'Bliss.' " *Twentieth Century Literature* 32 (Summer 1986): 242–54.

O'Sullivan, Vincent. "The Magnetic Chain: Notes and Approaches to K.M." *Landfall* 29 (June 1975): 95–131. Analysis of the influence of Wilde and Pater on Mansfield's technique and personality. Perceptive use of Turnbull manuscripts.

Waldron, Philip. "Katherine Mansfield's Journal." *Twentieth Century Literature* 20 (January 1974): 11–18. Exposes falsification in Murry's editing.

Wright, Celeste T. "Darkness as a Symbol in Katherine Mansfield." *Modern Philology* 51 (February 1954): 204–07. A study of tunnels and dark waters as obsessive symbols, rising from childhood fear of darkness.

———. "Genesis of a Short Story." *Modern Philology* 34 (January 1955): 91–96. Fly images before "The Fly."

———. "Katherine Mansfield's Boat Image." *Twentieth Century Literature* 1 (Oct. 1955): 128–32.

Index

The Author

From 1962 until 1988—when she was there—Saralyn Daly taught medieval and contemporary literature, linguistics, and writing at California State University, Los Angeles. Holding a Ph.D. from Ohio State University, she has taught at 12 universities, ranging from Bujumbura, Burundi, to Beirut; Texas to Tokyo; Kansas to Tübingen; and Aix-en-Provence to Ottawa. She has usually managed to drag Mansfield into it. In 1980 her verse translation, *The Book of True Love* (*Libro de Buen Amor,* by Juan Ruiz, Old Spanish text edited by A. N. Zahareas), won the Harold Morton Landon Prize, awarded by the Academy of American Poets. She has published scholarly articles, poetry, short stories, and two novels.